P9-CDY-394

HOW THINGS WORK

COMPUTERS

Other publications:

AMERICAN COUNTRY

VOYAGE THROUGH THE UNIVERSE

THE THIRD REICH

THE TIME-LIFE GARDENER'S GUIDE

MYSTERIES OF THE UNKNOWN

TIME FRAME

FIX IT YOURSELF

FITNESS, HEALTH & NUTRITION

SUCCESSFUL PARENTING

HEALTHY HOME COOKING

UNDERSTANDING COMPUTERS

LIBRARY OF NATIONS

THE ENCHANTED WORLD

THE KODAK LIBRARY OF CREATIVE PHOTOGRAPHY

GREAT MEALS IN MINUTES

THE CIVIL WAR

PLANET EARTH

COLLECTOR'S LIBRARY OF THE CIVIL WAR

THE EPIC OF FLIGHT

THE GOOD COOK

WORLD WAR II

HOME REPAIR AND IMPROVEMENT

THE OLD WEST

COVER

A composite image illustrating the emerging technologies that enable artists to marry conventional photography and computer-generated art. The image was assembled with Adobe Photoshop® by combining the photograph of a computer with three-dimensional geometrical objects created with StrataVision 3d®.

HOW THINGS WORK

COMPUTERS

TIME-LIFE BOOKS

ALEXANDRIA, VIRGINIA

Library of Congress Cataloging-in-Publication Data

Computers
      p.   cm. – (How things work)
    Includes index.
    ISBN 0-8094-7858-7
    ISBN 0-8094-7859-5
    1. Computers
    I. Time-Life Books. II. Series.
    QA76.5.C6C61384 1990
    004—dc20   90-47450
                         CIP

How Things Work was produced by
ST. REMY PRESS

PRESIDENT	Pierre Léveillé
PUBLISHER	Kenneth Winchester

Staff for *COMPUTERS*

Editor	Matthew Cope
Art Director	Philippe Arnoldi
Assistant Editor	Hugh Wilson
Contributing Editor	Bryce S. Walker
Research Editor	Fiona Gilsenan
Researcher	Hayes Jackson
Picture Editor	Chris Jackson
Designers	Chantal Bilodeau, Luc Germain
Illustrators	Maryse Doray, Nicolas Moumouris, Robert Paquet, Maryo Proulx
Index	Christine M. Jacobs

Staff for *HOW THINGS WORK*

Series Editor	Carolyn Jackson
Senior Art Director	Diane Denoncourt
Senior Editor	Elizabeth Cameron
Administrator	Natalie Watanabe
Production Manager	Michelle Turbide
Coordinator	Dominique Gagné
Systems Coordinator	Jean-Luc Roy

Time-Life Books Inc. is a wholly owned subsidiary of
THE TIME INC. BOOK COMPANY

President and Chief Executive Officer	Kelso F. Sutton
President, Time Inc. Books Direct	Christopher T. Linen

TIME-LIFE BOOKS INC.

EDITOR	George Constable
Director of Design	Louis Klein
Director of Editorial Resources	Phyllis K. Wise
Director of Photography and Research	John Conrad Weiser
PRESIDENT	John M. Fahey Jr.
Senior Vice Presidents	Robert M. DeSena, Paul R. Stewart, Curtis G. Viebranz, Joseph J. Ward
Vice Presidents	Stephen L. Bair, Bonita L. Boezeman, Mary P. Donohoe, Stephen L. Goldstein, Juanita T. James, Andrew P. Kaplan, Trevor Lunn, Susan J. Maruyama, Robert H. Smith
New Product Development	Trevor Lunn, Donia Ann Steele
Supervisor of Quality Control	James King
PUBLISHER	Joseph J. Ward

Editorial Operations

Production	Celia Beattie
Library	Louise D. Forstall
Correspondents	Elisabeth Kraemer-Singh (Bonn); Christina Lieberman (New York); Maria Vincenza Aloisi (Paris); Ann Natanson (Rome).

THE WRITERS

Dónal Kevin Gordon is a Vermont-based freelance writer. He has written previously for Time-Life Books, working on the *Mysteries of the Unknown, Understanding Computers* and *The Third Reich* among other series.

Peter Pocock is a freelance writer with a special interest in science and technology. He was a writer and editor for Time-Life Books for 10 years and most recently worked on the *Understanding Computers* and *Voyage Through the Universe* series. He also edited a series of manuals on personal computers for Time-Life in 1984, and is currently writing a novel.

Bruce F. Webster is the director of product development at Pages Software in San Diego. He is also a computer journalist who has written for *BYTE* and is the author of *The NeXT Book*. He earned his B.Sc in computer science from Brigham Young University.

THE CONSULTANTS

Ken Fogel is a professional consultant and professor of computer science at Dawson College in Montreal. He has designed computer systems for applications ranging from human resources to satellite tracking.

Michael R. Williams is a professor of computer science at the University of Calgary who has a particular interest in the history of computing. He earned a PhD in computer science from the University of Glasgow. During 1986 he was the Historian/Curator for the Computer Revolution project at the Smithsonian Institute in Washington, DC.

Dennis Allen, is a senior editor at *BYTE* magazine where he coordinates product reviews for the BYTE lab. Previously he was a senior editor for *Popular Computing.*

For information about any Time-Life book,
please write:
Reader Information
Time-Life Customer Service
P.O. Box C-32068
Richmond, Virginia
23261-2068

© 1990 Time-Life Books Inc. All rights reserved.
No part of this book may be reproduced in any form or by any electronic or mechanical means, including information storage and retrieval devices or systems, without prior written permission from the publisher, except that brief passages may be quoted for reviews.
First printing. Printed in U.S.A.
Published simultaneously in Canada.
School and library distribution by Silver Burdett Company, Morristown, New Jersey.

TIME-LIFE is a trademark of Time Warner Inc. U.S.A.

CONTENTS

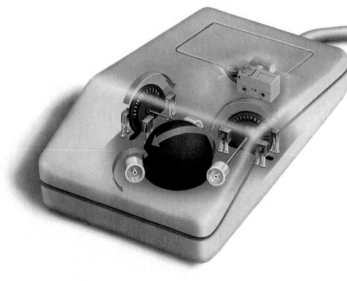

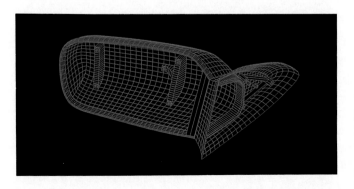

72 FOLLOWING INSTRUCTIONS

110 OUTPUT

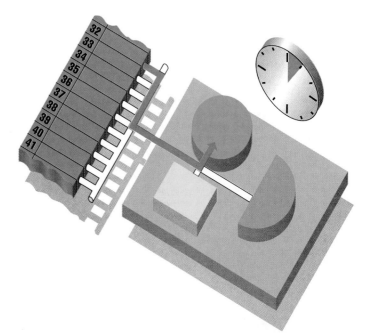

94 STORAGE

132 FUTURE CONSIDERATIONS

Beginnings

In the beginning, mathematics was not necessary at all. The most important thing primitive people needed to know about any quantity was whether the number involved was one, or many. But as nomadic tribes came together to form societies, more complex numbering systems had to be devised to meet the needs of agriculture, trade, navigation and organized economies.

The decimal system was a natural. People have 10 fingers, and they tend to count on them. But it was by no means the only option: The Babylonians, for example, developed a system based on the number 60 at least four millennia ago. The 60-second minute, the 60-minute hour and the 360-degree circle are all vestiges of this method.

Manipulating very large numbers in any system is beyond the mental capacity of most people. What was needed, then as now, was a painless means of producing an accurate result, while keeping track of intermediate calculations. The simple expedient of making marks in the dirt and using pebbles as counters was the earliest form of the abacus—and the first of many steps along the road to the computer.

As the centuries passed, mathematics saw such important breakthroughs as the invention of the concept of zero in India around A.D. 800, and the widespread adoption in Europe of the Hindu-Arabic numbers still in use today. These two developments meant that every conceivable number could be represented by a combination of the digits one through nine, plus zero. And they could be written down in columns corresponding to their positions on the abacus.

The first true calculating device (used to predict lunar eclipses) was invented by a 14th-Century Moslem mathematician named Al-Kashi. It consisted of a pair of hand-operated sliding disks marked with numbers, and was manipulated in much the same way as a slide rule. The 17th Century saw the introduction of John Napier's device for multiplying large numbers. But while Al-Kashi's mechanism and Napier's Bones *(far right)* were ingenious and elegantly simple, among their many drawbacks was the fact that they were not designed to keep a record of their work. Any new calculation erased the previous one.

The five fingers of each hand are undeniably convenient for counting and gave rise to the 10-digit decimal system.

The astrolabe was used by 14th-Century astronomers to measure the altitude of the stars and planets, and by navigators to calculate their position and course.

The rod-and-bead abacus, a Chinese invention, is still in wide use as a counting device. The rods correspond to columns and the beads to specific numbers.

John Napier, baron of Merchiston, Scotland, published a seminal paper in 1614 announcing his invention of logarithms, but in his own lifetime he was better known for the invention of this device. Napier's Bones were a hand-operated set of rods for performing multiplications involving large numbers.

Blaise Pascal built his first calculator (above) *in the mid-17th Century to help his father in his work as the tax commissioner of Upper Normandy. The machine became such a popular success that counterfeit Pascalines soon came onto the market.*

Herman Hollerith's tabulator was the first calculating machine to be successful in the wide-scale application to a practical problem: conducting the 1890 United States census. Data was entered on punched cards the size of dollar bills.

Charles Babbage never completed his Difference Engine, but his work, started in 1823, did prove that a machine could do a lot more than add, subtract and perform simple multiplications and divisions.

In 1643 a brilliant young French mathematician, Blaise Pascal, offered for sale to the public "a small machine of my own invention, by means of which you. . . may perform all the operations of arithmetic, and may be relieved of the work which has often times fatigued your spirit."

Pascal has been widely regarded as the father of mechanical calculators, but while his Pascaline was original, ingenious and influential, it was not the first machine of its kind. Wilhelm Schickard, an obscure German professor, built the first calculator with an internal mechanism for automatically performing carries in 1623, the year Pascal was born. But it was the Pascaline that rose to prominence, although despite its mechanical genius and its enthusiastic advertising claims, the machine and its immediate successors were little more than adding machines. Calculations of square roots, cube roots, interest rates and exponential functions called for something more sophisticated. That something was the Difference Engine invented by the Englishman Charles Babbage in 1823. Powered by a steam engine and a system of weights, the contraption would print out its results and keep calculations in a rudimentary form of storage. Although the Difference Engine was never developed beyond the working model stage, it offered a tantalizing hint of the potential of machines to take some of the drudgery out of intellectual work performed by humans.

At the core of the modern computer is the silicon chip. Cut from circular wafers like the one at right, chips are made up of thousands of electronic switches and circuits too small to be seen with the naked eye.

The Electronic Numerical Integrator And Computer was unveiled on 14 February 1946. Eighty feet long, 10 feet high and 3 feet deep, it tipped the scales at 30 tons. With thousands of vacuum tubes acting as switches, ENIAC was more than a thousand times faster than any previous computer. It was used to calculate the trajectories of artillery shells and to produce aiming tables for soldiers.

The first personal computers were the province of electronic hobbyists and amateur enthusiasts. By the 1990s, personal computers packed more power than their mainframe predecessors of only a few years earlier, and could be found in offices and homes all over the world.

The modern electronic computer was not the invention of any one person nor the result of a single technical breakthrough. It evolved from a number of machines built in Germany, England and the United States in the 1930s and 1940s, and its most important impetus came from military needs during World War II.

The computers of the 1950s and 1960s were large, expensive machines serving corporations and government. Though the quest was, as it still is, for smaller, faster and more affordable machines, nobody really envisioned a mass demand for home computers until the end of the 1970s.

Even Steven Jobs and Stephen Wozniak thought their prototype home product, the Apple I, would appeal only to a limited market of hobbyists called hackers. Their first commercially available machine, the

Apple II, was introduced in 1977 and cost $1,195—a price that did not include a monitor. IBM introduced its personal computer, the PC, in 1981, setting off a corporate rivalry that shows no sign of abating.

In the last 50 years, computers have penetrated every imaginable facet of life. To generations that grew up without them, computers can appear miraculous, mysterious and sometimes intimidating. To the generation that came of age with them, computers are commonplace—an undeniable part of everyday life. Where computerization might lead is a matter for speculation. But how the machines work is a fascinating mix of theory, technology and applied science.

THE EVERYDAY MIRACLE

Some say the computer is simply a tool for solving problems, and that there is nothing miraculous about it. If so, it is surely the most versatile tool yet devised by human ingenuity. What other machine—with no special modifications—can be used one day to write a symphony, and the next to dispatch a spacecraft far beyond the limits of the solar system? Identical computers, running different programs, can be used to handle the payroll of a small business, or to make financial projections for an entire national economy. A computer may draw a precise map of a patient's heart to guide a surgeon's knife, or paint the dazzling special effects of a feature film. Unseen computers routinely perform such tasks as monitoring traffic, checking grocery prices or controlling telephone networks. A new generation of smaller, cheaper machines has moved onto millions of desktops to help with such everyday tasks as balancing bank accounts, producing error-free correspondence and teaching children.

The technological discoveries and inventions that have made civilization possible are relatively few in number. With the taming of fire and the invention of the wheel, prehistoric tribes took a giant step from the uncertainties of a nomadic, foraging way of life toward a more ordered existence. Astronomers learned to measure the movement of the stars, and their calendars calculated the punctual arrival of the seasons. With predictable cycles of planting and harvesting, and the domestication of animals, city-states could arise. Monetary systems became the foundation of trade. Numbering systems and bureaucracies kept track of business transactions and inventory control for food supplies. Censuses were taken, and the figures used for taxation and property records. Despite the dizzying advances of 20th-Century technology, the lineage of modern computers wends through generations of calculators, stretching back thousands of years. Traces of the earliest calculator—the table abacus—have been unearthed from the ruins of ancient

Across the ages, societies have produced artifacts that define their technological achievements. The small disk at left, believed to be a form of calendar, is from the Minoan palace of Phaistos, and dates back to 1700 B.C. The Stone of the Sun in the center is a 500-year-old history of the world known to the Aztecs. The wafer of chips at right has been cut from a cylinder of silicon, and forms the core of computer technology.

Babylon. This simple apparatus gave merchants a calculating device so efficient that a later form of it—the rod and bead abacus—is still in use in many countries today. By the 17th Century, mathematicians and mechanics began to devise equipment that could meet the computational demands of sciences such as physics and astronomy. Ever more sophisticated machines appeared in their workshops and notebooks. Assemblages of gears, cogs, axles and springs were devised in an effort to reduce the amount of time required for extensive mathematical calculations. These machines were limited by the materials and technology available at the time.

The development of the printing press, firearms, the steam engine and the production line all hastened the march toward mechanization, as mass production led toward an industrial society. The historically recent arrival of the internal combustion engine, the telephone, the airplane, radio and television have opened channels of communication and transportation that can span the world in fractions of a second. As momentous as each of these advancements has been, they may all yet be eclipsed by the measureless potential of the computer.

The limitless spectrum of computer applications sometimes masks the true nature of this lightning logician. Stripped to its barest essentials, a computer is an astonishingly fast calculator, all of its circuits constantly coursing with coded bursts of electricity. Millions of interconnected switches open and close millions of times each second. Pulses of current weave the intricate tapestries of logic that underlie the computer's every action. The fundamental operations of the computer —adding, subtracting and comparing numbers—are relatively simple. Complexity and diversity arise from the myriad ways those operations are combined to produce

WORKING IN CONCERT

A computer system is made up of many different components working in concert. In this typical layout external input and output devices are connected to the system unit.

The scanner translates visual material into a numerical form that the computer can process.

The most common input device is the keyboard. It converts keystrokes into the numerical language of computing.

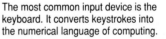

The modem permits computers to use ordinary telephone lines to communicate with other computers.

Removable floppy disks hold programs and data files.

results that may have no immediately apparent connection to mathematics. Colorful graphics, the words of a letter or a poem, the notes of a musical score—all are reduced to numbers, for processing in the arithmetical nucleus of the computer.

The circuits that make up that nucleus are stacked in strata on microchips—tiny slivers of silicon that can be smaller than a baby's fingernail. The product of a whirlwind electronic revolution, microchips are the main driving force behind today's proliferation of computers.

THE ESSENTIALS

UNIVAC, the first commercial computer, was used to predict the outcome of the 1952 United States presidential election. A modern desktop computer is only a fraction the size of its illustrious predecessor, but its essential elements are virtually identical. It uses input devices to accept data and programs; output devices to present information to the user. Inside the cabinet a central processing unit (CPU) manipulates data and controls the computer. An electronic memory stores instructions, information, intermediate calculations and results.

Today the standard input device is the keyboard, adapted from typewriter design. The two most common output devices are the video screen and the printer. Some equipment combines both input and output functions. A touch-screen, for example, accepts commands, and instantly displays the result. Another common input-output device is the modem (short for modulator-demodulator), which translates computer data to and from the format required to send it over telephone lines.

All instructions arrive at the CPU's control unit, which interprets them and flashes signals that set the computer's circuits to execute the task at hand. All the math-

The display of output on the screen—the most common output device—enables the user to interact with the computer.

The mouse allows the user to select commands from the screen.

The printer gives the user a hard copy of the computer's output on paper.

ematical and logical work is handled by another part of the CPU, the arithmetic logic unit (ALU), which receives numbers from memory. Based on its instructions from the control unit, the ALU adds, divides, compares or performs some other manipulation of the numbers. New orders from the control unit direct the disposition of the results, sending them to memory, to the screen, to some other output device or to a storage device. Among the most common are magnetic disk or tape drives where information and instructions can be stored and retrieved as needed.

The driving force behind all this electronic processing and storage are silicon microchips called integrated circuits. In desktop computers, one chip called a microprocessor contains the entire CPU. It is surrounded by other chips that perform the rest of the computer's basic functions. Read-only memory (ROM) chips hold permanent programs, usually installed by the computer manufacturer, that tell the microprocessor how to move and store data, and how to work with other parts of the machine. The computer's working memory resides in chips of another sort, called read-and-write memory, or RAM (the somewhat misleading acronym actually stands for random-access memory). RAM chips retain data only as long as the microprocessor needs it for the job at hand. Interface chips handle input

The power supply converts the AC power from a wall outlet into the DC voltages used by the computer.

Expansion slots allow the addition of a range of input and output devices.

The hard disk drive is a sealed unit with a nonremovable disk. It holds more information than a floppy disk, and access to the information is faster.

The flat motherboard is an assembly that contains the computer's integrated circuits and their connections.

The floppy disk drive is a device that reads and writes information on removable floppy disks.

and output, interpreting signals from such devices as the keyboard, and shaping the letters, numbers and images to display on a screen or print on paper. Other subsidiary chips are more specialized, acting as processors in their own right. These coprocessors take on jobs that might bog down the central processor, such as heavy mathematical calculations, manipulation of complex graphic images or generation of multichannel sound for musical arrangements.

No matter how powerful and flexible its electronics may be, a computer cannot function without instructions called programs. It is the programs that transform the computer into a word processor, a flight simulator, an electronic bookkeeper or an arcade game. The programs are called software, to distinguish their ephemeral nature from the solid physicality of the equipment, or hardware. A program is nothing more than a list of very detailed instructions that tell the computer how to respond to any situation that may arise as it performs the designated job. Computer software is encoded in a special language of numbers that corresponds to the internal makeup of the machine, with its millions of electronic switches.

INSIDE THE CHIP

The essential elements of microchips, switches called transistors, are microscopically small electronic components that can amplify an electrical current, or switch it on or off, by allowing its passage or blocking its flow. Switches are said to be open or closed, although in fact current continues to flow through the entire system at all times, so the switches are never completely closed. But for all practical purposes such switches have a two-state nature, which makes them perfectly suited to handle the only language a computer understands: binary numbers. In the binary system, all numbers are represented by combinations of just two digits—zero and one. Working with only two states, the binary code may not at first seem capable of any great subtlety or complexity. Yet, amazingly, these two binary building blocks—a one and a zero—establish the entire foundation for all facets of computing. When a low-voltage current is applied to a switch, it is read as a zero. A high-voltage current represents a one. Any switch, therefore, can stand for a single binary digit, or bit, the basic unit of measurement in computing. Computer scientists describe the functioning of a machine in terms of multiples of bits, (eight bits make a byte, 1,024 bytes are called a kilobyte, or K, and 1,048,576 bytes are called a megabyte, or Mb), but the elemental binary digit underlies everything.

In a computer circuit, a transistor is used to block the flow of current or let it pass, allowing the circuit to express the binary language of information processing. Switches can be connected to each other in a variety of ways to make circuits called logic gates. Just three kinds of logic gates combine to perform addition, subtraction, multiplication division or comparison of numbers and symbols. Etched into the silicon and metal of computer circuits, the rules of logic allow the manipulation of information, expressed as binary numbers.

The earliest computers used switches that were larger and slower than transistors. The first such devices were built with electro-mechanical relays borrowed from the telephone industry. The relays used magnetism, triggered by a low-voltage current, to open or close a gap in a circuit. Slow but reliable, the thousands of relays in early computers set up an incessant clatter as they worked. One observer compared the sound to a "roomful of old ladies knitting away with steel needles."

INSIDE THE BOX

The internal components of the personal computer shown at left include a power supply, input and output ports, circuit boards and disk drives. The layout of these elements varies from manufacturer to manufacturer. Many of the components are modular, and the computer can be customized according to the user's needs.

Relays, however, were soon superseded by vacuum tubes, which had no moving parts and controlled the flow of electricity only by electrical forces.

The vacuum tubes most commonly used in computers at that time are called triodes—a reference to the three basic elements housed inside a glass bulb from which the air has been removed. The first element is the cathode, a wire filament that is heated cherry-red by an external power source until it emits electrons, which carry a negative charge. The electrons surge through the vacuum to the second element, a metal plate called the anode, completing the circuit and allowing a current to flow from cathode to anode. The third element in the tube is a metal grid between the cathode and the anode. If a negative charge is applied to the grid, it repels the electrons from the cathode, so that they cannot reach the anode. In this case, the circuit remains broken and no current flows.

Although vacuum tubes were hundreds or thousands of times faster than the electromechanical relays, they had serious shortcomings. The thousands of tubes necessary in a large computer generated prodigious amounts of heat, despite the presence of cooling fans. One early computer called ENIAC sometimes raised the temperature in its room to 120 degrees F. The air-conditioning systems required to control such heat sometimes consumed as much electricity as the tubes themselves. Furthermore, vacuum tubes were less reliable than relays, since they were prone to burning out like light bulbs. In fact, it happened so frequently that technicians with carts full of spare tubes had to patrol the machine, constantly ready to perform on-the-spot maintenance.

THE TRANSISTOR BREAKTHROUGH

Transistors brought an end to these problems. Invented in 1947, they were small, reliable, cool and efficient in their use of electricity. Although they quickly became ubiquitous in a wide variety of electronic applications ranging from hearing aids to radios, transistors were not used in computers on a regular basis until the late 1950s. The first designs used junction transistors, tiny sandwiches of materials called semiconductors. Semiconductors are a small class of substances with unusual electrical properties: Under some conditions they conduct electricity, while under others they do not. Other materials generally fall into one of two categories: insulators such as rubber or glass, which always block the flow of electricity, and conductors such as copper and aluminum, which always allow a current to flow with little constraint.

The materials most commonly used in early transistors were germanium and silicon, crystalline substances that in their pure form act as insulators. However, when combined with tiny amounts of impurities (in a process known as doping), germanium and silicon do permit the passage of electricity. The way the impurity, or dopant, fits into the semiconductor's crystalline framework determines the way that it carries electricity. Each atom of the dopant may provide the structure with an extra electron, in which case the material conducts current in the ordinary way, as a flow of negatively charged electrons. Some dopants, however, produce a deficiency of electrons, leaving so-called electron holes. These holes migrate through the material in the same way electrons do, carrying a positive charge. This kind of material is called a p-type semiconductor. Its counterpart, carrying a negative charge, is called n-type.

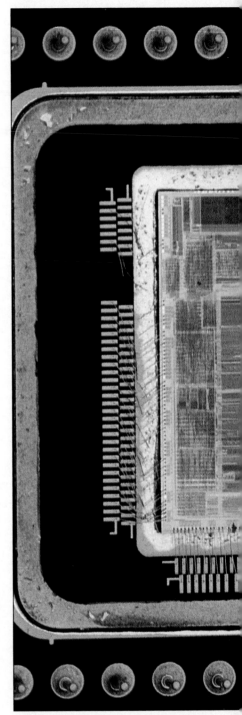

The microprocessor chip is the core of all personal computers. This state-of-the-art Intel i486 packs 1,180,235 transistors onto a silicon chip measuring .414 by .649 inches.

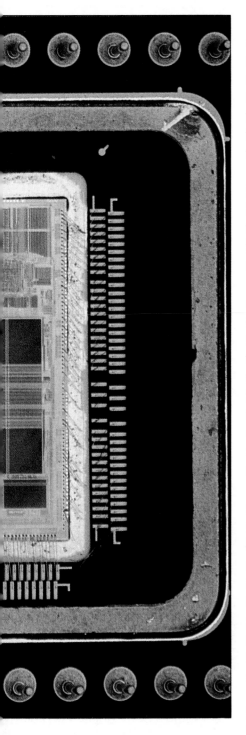

The early junction transistor was a composite assembly, with a slice of p-type material, called the base, layered between two slices of n-type material, the emitter and the collector. At the junctions between the p-type base and the n-type emitter and collector, a complex electrical phenomenon produces nonconductive regions called depletion areas. Ordinarily, the depletion areas are too wide to allow current to flow from emitter to collector. But the application of a positive control current to the base shrinks the depletion areas, permitting the passage of current. Like a triode, the junction transistor could then work as an electrically controlled switch.

A standard junction transistor, housed in a protective canister about one-quarter inch in diameter and one-quarter inch long, was far smaller than the vacuum tube it replaced. It was extremely reliable and generated little heat. By the late 1950s, transistorized computers began to appear in the marketplace. They were smaller, faster, cheaper, more dependable and far more powerful than their predecessors, and soon had the field to themselves.

Transistors had drawbacks of their own, however. The semiconductors were connected to circuits by wires that had to be soldered in place. As computer designers developed ever more complicated circuits, the sheer volume of connections began to erode the reliability of their machines. Even though the transistors themselves were nearly immune to failure, it was increasingly likely that somewhere in the maze of soldered wires a connection would come loose, bringing the computer to grief. Furthermore, the miniaturization initiated by transistors had whetted designers' appetites. They began to envision enormously powerful machines with millions of components. Even with transistors, these devices took up an impractical amount of space. The solution to these problems eventually emerged from continued semiconductor research.

In 1958 Jack Kilby, an electrical engineer at Texas Instruments, realized that with silicon he could make not only transistors, but also such circuit elements as resistors, which impede the flow of current, and capacitors, which hold a charge. It would be relatively simple, Kilby concluded, to make all the components of a circuit on a single piece of semiconductor. Within months, he had fashioned a crude prototype that was the world's first integrated circuit, or IC. It was a thin slice of germanium less than a half-inch long, incorporating five separate components linked to each other by tiny wires. As Kilby assembled other, more complex ICs, the potential for miniaturization became clear; his patent application claimed that ICs could reduce the space requirements for electronic circuits by a factor of 60.

Texas Instruments had little commercial success with Kilby's ICs. The wires used to connect the components made them difficult to manufacture and relatively unreliable. Other researchers, however, were working on similar ideas, based on a new kind of junction transistor introduced in late 1958 by physicist Jean Hoerni at Fairchild Semiconductors in California. Instead of building up a sandwich with alternating layers of p-type and n-type semiconductor, Hoerni devised a technique for embedding the layers, nested inside each other like mixing bowls, in a single piece of silicon. He covered the transistor with a thin coating of silicon dioxide—an excellent insulator—leaving tiny holes in the protective layer where electrical leads could be connected to the edges of each of the bowl-shaped layers. Called a planar transistor because its surface was flat, Hoerni's device proved more reliable than previous types of junction transistors. The planar transistor was also cheaper, since it was well suited to mass production. Many transistors were fabricated simultaneously on a single wafer of silicon, and then cut apart. In the next step, individual transistors were wired together in different configurations for different purposes.

In 1959 Hoerni's colleague Robert Noyce took planar transistors one step further. He realized that instead of cutting apart the multiple transistors on a silicon wafer, he could build other electrical components into the semiconductor, integrating all the pieces of a complete circuit. Noyce also devised a way to connect the electronic elements by laying down thin layers of metal that contacted the semiconductor only through the holes etched in the silicon dioxide insulating layer. This was far more efficient than using wires, which, until this development, had to be attached by hand under a microscope. Noyce's techniques became the basis of modern integrated circuit manufacture.

By 1962, both Fairchild and Texas Instruments were producing ICs based on Noyce's methods. Chips, as the tiny wafers came to be called, were in demand not only for computers, but also for any devices that needed compact, reliable circuitry, from electronic calculators to missile guidance systems. Technological advances allowed manufacturers to pack more and more components onto a single chip. The number of components on a chip a tenth of an inch square increased

SWITCHES: MINIATURIZATION = SPEED

The four devices shown from left to right are all switches. Electro-mechanical relays were used in the computers of the 1940s. Vacuum tubes soon replaced the bulky—and balky—magnetic relays, but had problems of their own. Transistors were smaller, faster and cooler than their predecessors, and the arrival of the integrated circuit combined thousands of transistors into a single component. With each new incarnation, switches became smaller, therefore current traveled shorter distances. As a result, each generation of switches was faster than its predecessor.

from 10 in 1964 to 1,000 in 1970. This degree of miniaturization also made the chip's operations faster, since electrical impulses, moving near the speed of light, had to travel shorter distances measured in mere hundred-thousandths of an inch. Computer manufacturers did not begin to incorporate chips into their machines on a large scale until the mid-1960s. This was not a simple process, since logic circuits had to be completely redesigned to accommodate the new technology.

MEMORIES ARE MADE OF THIS

Just as chip technology transformed logic circuitry, it also revolutionized memory. Before chips—and long before the advent of the desktop computer—most computers used magnetic-core memories, wire grids strung with thousands of tiny ceramic ferrite rings, or cores; each core could hold just one bit, a zero or a one. The cores required to hold one kilobyte of data—approximately 200 five-letter words—took up about 80 square inches. But to be really useful, a computer needs to be able to store many thousands of words. Using this system, a typical home computer of today would require a memory device that takes up 200 cubic feet.

The first 1K memory chip was a significant breakthrough. Developed by Intel (a chip-making company founded by Robert Noyce), it was introduced in 1970. It was housed in a holder only about a seventh of an inch long, which allowed computer manufacturers to build far smaller machines. Computers made with the new chips were more reliable and used less space and electricity, but most important, they provided hundreds of times the computing power at significantly lower prices, further spurring the growth of the industry.

In 1971, Intel brought out another even more remarkable semiconductor device, a chip called the 4004—the first microprocessor. Designed by a young engineer named Ted Hoff, it was a single processor that combined the capabilities of arithmetic and logic circuits usually built as separate chips. The 4004 had 2,250 transistors, arranged so that the chip could be programmed to execute a wide variety of tasks. Although it was designed to run an electronic calculator, the chip could actually perform all the functions of a computer's central processing unit. In fact, a designer had only to connect a 4004 with other chips for memory, control and input-output to produce a machine as powerful as some large computers of the 1950s.

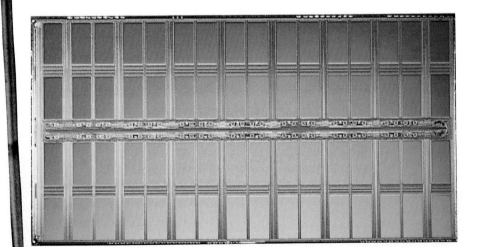

Dozens of competitors soon joined Intel in the marketplace. Their customers were not only computer companies, but also manufacturers of all kinds of products that could benefit from built-in processing, from household appliances to cars to industrial robots. Nevertheless, microprocessors did have a significant impact on the computer business, serving as the central processors for an entirely new category of machines called personal computers—inexpensive and compact devices that would bring the benefits of computing to millions of homes and offices over the next two decades.

The 4004 could add two four-digit binary numbers in an astonishing eleven millionths of a second. Larger numbers had to be broken down into four-bit pieces, then reconstituted after processing in the arithmetic logic unit. In 1974 Intel introduced the 8080, which processed data in eight-bit chunks. It could add two of the larger numbers in a quarter of the time. A year later a small company called MOS Technology brought out a chip called the 6502. Cheap and very fast, it could add two eight-bit numbers in just a millionth of a second. The 8080 and the 6502, both sporting more than 4,000 components, quickly became standards for the personal computer industry, which took off with the introduction of the Apple II and the Commodore PET.

Computer makers soon found the limits of the early microprocessors. Their eight-bit data paths were still a bottleneck (the largest decimal number that can be expressed with eight binary digits is 255), and a large portion of their circuitry was devoted to the complex task of organizing the work, leaving less space for processing. The answer was to squeeze more elements onto a chip. But this raised new problems. The primary issue was the rising temperature of denser chips. Some of the power coursing through a circuit is always converted into heat. More components consumed more power, sometimes generating enough heat to burn out the chip. Stopgap measures such as refrigeration were costly and cumbersome. The real solution would be a new type of transistor that gave off less heat.

The basic science needed to surmount the heat barrier had been around for decades, in the form of the MOS transistor (MOS stands for metal-oxide-semiconductor, the three major ingredients). Unlike standard planar transistors, a MOS transistor uses no power when it is switched off; consequently its overall power consumption is much lower, and it produces less heat. It is also simpler and cheaper to manufacture than other transistors. Developing the technology, however, proved extremely difficult, since MOS transistors require the utmost purity in the silicon dioxide coating used as insulation between layers on the chips. Years of research finally yielded methods for producing uniformly pure layers of silicon dioxide, and MOS-based chips began to appear in the early 1970s.

Because MOS transistors put out so little heat, far more of them could be crammed onto a chip without the need for sophisticated cooling systems. The increasing density of integration allowed circuits with tens of thousands of elements arranged in as many as 15 layers on a single chip. In 1979 Motorola introduced the 68000 microprocessor, with 70,000 components. It handled data in 16-bit pieces, and was powerful enough to do multiplication as a single operation, rather than as a series of additions. The 68000 was blindingly fast. It could multiply two 16-bit numbers in 3.2 millionths of a second. It was soon eclipsed, however. In 1981, Hewlett-Packard brought out a 450,000-component superchip, the first 32-

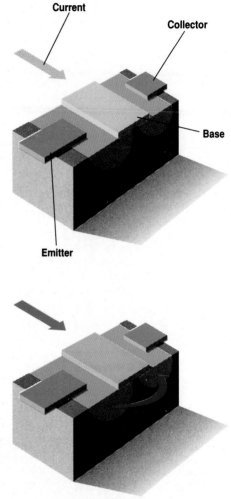

HOW TRANSISTORS WORK

The transistor shown above is a type of switch. When a weak electrical current flows through the base, the current entering through the emitter is prevented from reaching the collector, and the switch is off (top). Increasing the current to the base (bottom) allows the flow of current to the collector, and turns the switch on.

CLOSING IN ON THE CHIP

The large photograph *(above)* shows a scanning electron microscope's view of an array of switches in a four-megabit RAM chip, magnified 2,000 times actual size. The photograph at right shows a single switch from the same chip magnified 12,000 times. There are 4,096,000 such switches in the chip.

bit microprocessor. More powerful than the central processors of many contemporary mainframe computers, it could handle decimal numbers larger than 3.2 billion as single entities, and multiply them in 1.8 millionths of a second.

SMALLER, DENSER, FASTER

The early microchips were thumbtack-small, lightning-fast and crammed with circuitry, or "dense" in the parlance of the trade. But smaller, faster, denser chips were the order of the day, and within a few years the technology of Large Scale Integration, or LSI, made it possible to compress thousands of circuits onto a single chip. Hot on LSI's heels came VLSI, or Very Large Scale Integration, which allowed hundreds of thousands of individual components to be chemically etched into the layers of a chip just 4/1,000 of an inch thick. By 1989 the first chips to break the million-transistor barrier were rolling out of the sterile "clean rooms" of California's Silicon Valley, south of San Francisco.

Like all advances, however, VLSI raised new problems for chip makers. The circuitry for the Hewlett-Packard chip was so complex that it took a team of engineers 18 months to design. The plans, plotted on four-by-eight-foot sheets of drafting paper, would cover the floor of a large gymnasium. The enormous task would have been impossible without the use of specialized computer programs to help map the millions of connections and check the accuracy of the final blueprint. A typical chip-design program includes a library of plans for the basic components, such as transistors, and subassemblies, such as memory cells. By pointing at objects on a screen and typing instructions, a designer can select the necessary elements and arrange them in circuits that will handle the binary data in the desired manner. Some programs can even design such a circuit layout, working from a diagram of the processes the designer wants the chip to perform.

But even with the most powerful design systems and precise manufacturing methods, the process of VLSI has limits. Electronic pathways can be whittled only so far before becoming so narrow that they run the risk of being destroyed by the very current they carry. Transistors smaller than bacteria operate on so little current that cosmic rays—high-speed atomic particles that bombard the Earth—can cause random switching errors. To overcome these and other obstacles to faster computing, some researchers have turned away from conventional semiconductor technology to investigate even more exotic kinds of switches.

It is worth remembering that as advanced as the electronic computer may appear, it is still only in its infancy. Making predictions beyond what is known to be in development is a speculative business at best. The computer industry has a habit of outstripping its own best-informed prophets with sometimes embarrassing regularity and rapidity. Some undeterred researchers, however, envisage a big future for logic circuits whose switches are operated not by electrical currents, but by pulses of light from microscopic lasers. Advances in such light computers are announced almost weekly, as the quest for higher speed and lower operating temperature leads away from silicon altogether. Other visionaries foresee developments in genetic engineering that will lead to bio-chips—pieces of organic material with billions of switches, each one a single protein molecule. Whatever the outcome of these research efforts, the present trend seems likely to continue: Computers will become faster, smaller, cheaper and ever more widespread.

The design of computer chips has become
yet another computer application. Work
once done on floor-sized blueprints is now
done on screen. The chip designer selects
elements from a "menu," and places them
into an intricate layout.

Layer Upon Layer . . .

They pour out by the millions a day, taking shape in automated, dust-proof workrooms from Japan to America—the newly minted microchips that are the building blocks of the computer revolution. Each one contains a three-dimensional labyrinth of microscopic circuitry, and anywhere from several thousand to four million switches, all built within a paper-thin sliver of silicon no larger than a thumbnail. Yet for all their delicacy and precision, they are a triumph of electronic mass production.

The fabrication process relies on the century-old technique of photolithography, still used for everyday printing jobs—including the production of this book. In chip manufacturing though, the process is millions of times more precise and is carried out by computer-driven robots and automated devices that allow for exacting miniaturization. And the assembly rooms in which the chips are produced are among the world's cleanest environments. No human hand ever touches a chip. Workers are clad head to toe in white "bunny suits" complete with masks, gloves and booties. Dust is the archenemy. Filtration systems cleanse the air, allowing no more than one .3-micron-wide dust particle per cubic foot into rooms a thousand times more sterile than a typical operating room. With individual switches measuring as little as 1/300 the width of a human hair, even a single smoke particle can destroy a chip in the making, blocking its circuits as effectively as a boulder blocks a highway.

The manufacture begins by reducing the circuit patterns on the chip-designer's screen to the size of the actual chip. Several painstaking steps are required. In any one chip the circuits are arranged in layers that are stacked one above the other; some chips contain as many as 18 different circuit layers. A separate photographic master plate is made for each layer. Then the image must be reduced still more with a step-and-repeat camera until it reaches its final size.

The final miniaturized master plate serves as the template for the creation of optically pure photomasks that will be used as stencils to create hundreds of identical chips. A spe-

KLA IMAGE COMPUTER

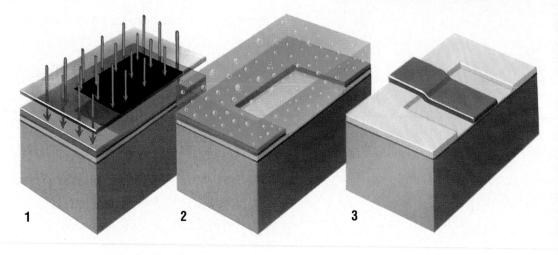

1   2   3

THE CHIPMAKER'S CRAFT

These simplified illustrations show some of the key steps in making chips. In step one, a silicon wafer is coated with a light-sensitive layer called photoresist, which is masked by a stencil and then exposed to ultraviolet light. The photoresist hardens in areas open to the light. Next, acids and solvents strip away the unexposed areas, baring the patterns of silicon that will be etched by superhot gases. In the third step, more silicon is laid down, masked and stripped as before.

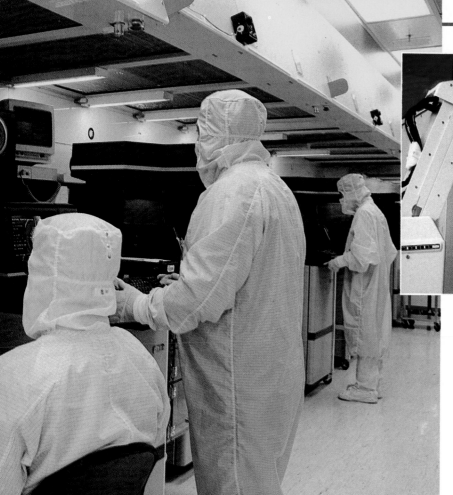

Chipmakers wear protective suits in sterile clean rooms (left). This is just one of many elaborate precautions taken to protect the chips from dust contamination. To prevent vibrations that could ruin chips during the fabrication process, the facilities are built on special waffle-shaped concrete foundations. A robot arm (above) loads silicon wafers into a special oxidization furnace where they will be coated with a thin layer of silicon dioxide.

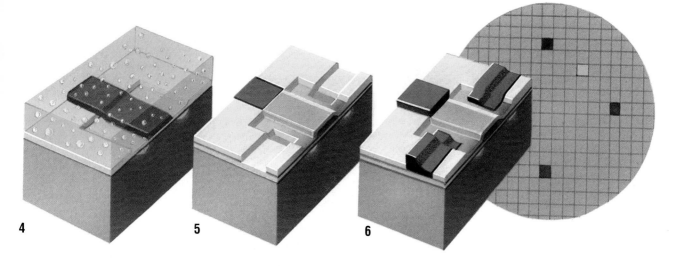

4   **5**   **6**

In the fourth step, the silicon is "doped" with chemical impurities to form positive and negative conducting zones. Step five shows the repetition of previous steps, building up layers on the chip that are linked by connecting "windows". In step

six, metal, often aluminum, is condensed onto the chip, filling gaps to form conducting pathways. When this is complete, all chips are tested and those that perform properly are cut from the circular silicon wafer to be packaged and wired for use.

At various stages in the manufacturing process the wafer is placed in a diffusion furnace (above). There high-temperature gases are applied to specified areas of the chips on the wafer, altering their electrical properties.

Each chip is tested before it is cut from the wafer. Probes are connected to contact pads built up during fabrication. A computer sends electrical signals into every chip and identifies any flawed components.

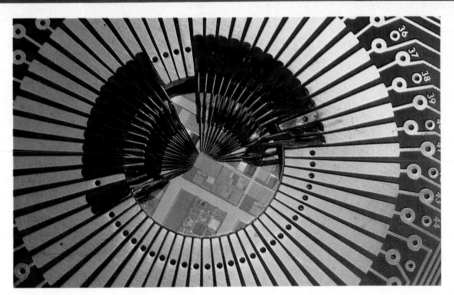

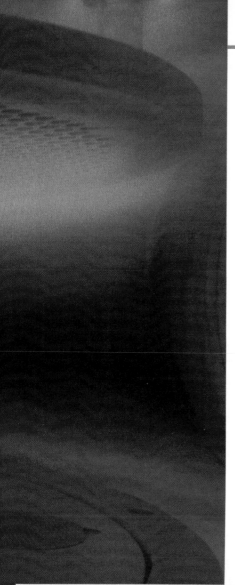

cial engraving tool sends a beam of electrons through the master plate and on to the photomask. The image registers the pattern of the base level circuits for the first chip. The beam shifts and prints the identical pattern for another chip. The process continues, row upon row, anywhere from 200 to 450 times depending on the size of the chip. The photomask is now ready to serve as a stencil for the first layer of circuitry in these chips.

Up to 200 fabrication steps will take place on a round, razor-thin silicon wafer in a process that can take from two to eight weeks, depending on the intricacy and power of the chips being made. The wafer is first coated with a layer of silicon dioxide, then topped with a light-sensitive chemical called photoresist. When ultraviolet light is projected through the pattern-bearing photomask its image is cast onto the resist, which hardens wherever the light hits. A series of acid baths washes away the resist—first the soft areas, then the hardened ones—along with part of the dioxide. What remains is the pattern of circuitry, etched in relief into the remaining areas of silicon dioxide.

In the next step a polysilicon compound is diffused in a furnace at ultra-high temperatures into the etched areas through a vaporization process. Specific areas of the circuitry are "doped" with impurities—either phosphorous, boron or arsenic—which enhance the polysilicon's conductivity.

With the first layer completed, another layer of photoresist is laid down and the chipmakers repeat the same procedure again and again, to build subsequent levels. Successive layers are overlaid, and slowly a three-dimensional structure of intricate, transecting electronic pathways is constructed. Each electrically active level is carefully insulated from the next level to prevent any possible short circuiting.

Finally, a thin sheet of metal topped with a glass-like protective coating is added to the surface of the chip. Openings are etched into this layer, revealing a series of bonding pads, or electrical contacts. Each chip is tested through the bonding pad. The wafer is then cut into its individual chips, which are encased in modules, or packages, for distribution throughout the world.

In the final stage of manufacture, after testing is complete, lasers cut the wafer into individual chips, ready for packaging.

INPUT

A t the height of World War II, scientists at the University of Pennsylvania were working against the clock to perfect what they hoped would be the world's fastest computing machine. The United States Army needed quick answers to certain problems in ballistics. Specifically, the Army wanted accurate mathematical guidelines for aiming and firing its new high-powered artillery guns. The university's 80-foot-long Electronic Numerical Integrator and Computer, ENIAC, was being readied to do just that. Completed too late to see wartime service, ENIAC was a mammoth assembly that incorporated 17,468 vacuum tubes and thousands of relays, resistors and capacitors. And ENIAC was undeniably fast. It could add 5,000 numbers in one second, and calculate a 30-second shell trajectory more quickly than the shell itself could fly from gun muzzle to target. But as fast as ENIAC was in processing, getting it to perform such feats was tedious in the extreme. For each new calculation, programmers had to spend hours plugging in thousands of feet of electronic cable and adjusting 6,000 switches one by one. Nor was this all. Before it could start crunching numbers, the computer had to digest data from a cumbersome aggregation of hundreds of punched cards.

Methods of input have improved immeasurably since the laborious days of ENIAC, but the computer's need for instructions and data remains the same. Most machinery, both electronic and mechanical, needs input. To supply the information that tells a car to power forward, the driver turns on the ignition, applies pressure to the gas pedal, and selects the correct gear. By the same token, a computer responds to information the user pours into it by means of various input devices.

Computers can process information from a multitude of sources—from keyboards and hand-held mechanisms called mice, from radio signals, from sensors that measure such things as air pressure and wind speed. Input can enter on beams of light and through musical notes, from arcade game joysticks, and even from

The touch of a finger can have far-reaching consequences. Depressing a key on a computer keyboard converts raw information into bits and bytes, and pours pulses of numerically coded information into the CPU through the input ports.

the touch of a finger on a display screen. Whatever the source, however, the information must be delivered in the only idiom a computer can understand—binary digits. A task of many input devices, therefore, is to translate incoming data into a sequence of bits and bytes.

THE LOGIC OF BINARY COMMUNICATION

The English statesman, philosopher and essayist Sir Francis Bacon (1561-1626) pioneered the binary idiom. Using only the letters A and B, he developed a cipher for encrypting secret diplomatic messages. By assigning a different five-unit sequence of As and Bs to each letter of the alphabet, Bacon was able to write any word he wished. The German philosopher and mathematician Gottfried Wilhelm von Leibniz (1646-1716) made a more direct contribution to the development of computer science when he formalized and perfected the combination of ones and zeros that make up the modern binary code.

The binary code expresses all numbers, of any size, as combinations of ones and zeros. The decimal number 43 seen below, for example, is written as 101011 in binary. For all its theoretical simplicity and orderliness, the binary code would be a hopelessly unwieldy and impractical system for everyday use. It is hard for people accustomed to the 10-based decimal system to distinguish one binary number from another; binary mental arithmetic would be an impossible nightmare.

DECIMAL		BINARY			
10	1	8	4	2	1
	0				0
	1				1
	2			1	0
	3			1	1
	4		1	0	0
	5		1	0	1
	6		1	1	0
	7		1	1	1
	8	1	0	0	0
	9	1	0	0	1
1	0	1	0	1	0

READING BINARY NUMBERS

Binary place columns increase by powers of two. Adding up the value of places marked by binary 1s gives the decimal equivalent. Thus, binary 101 equals decimal 5 (one 4 + one 1).

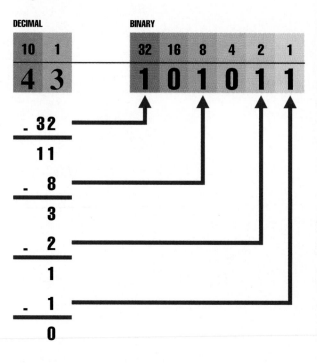

DECIMAL TO BINARY

To convert a decimal number to binary, first subtract the largest possible power of two, and keep subtracting each successive largest possible power, marking 1s in each column where this is possible, and 0s where it is not. For decimal 43; there is one 32, no 16, one 8, no 4, one 2 and one 1—yielding the binary number 101011.

But for computers, this two-based, one-or-zero binary system dovetails neatly into the nature of switches. A switch, like a light bulb, is a two-state device: It is, for all practical purposes, open or closed. Because of such simplicity, switches can perform any kind of computational task, when used to symbolize binary digits. In the computer's world view an open switch can represent a one, and a closed switch can stand for a zero.

One of the first practical applications of switch technology as input took place in the textile industry in 1804. The Frenchman Joseph Marie Jacquard (1752-1834) refined an existing technology for controlling looms with an arrangement of perforated cards in a moving loop. He may not have known it, but Jacquard was putting binary principles into practice, since the presence of each perforation was, in effect, a switch that was open. The absence of any perforation was a switch that was closed. Wooden plungers connected to different colored threads passed through the punched holes whenever they encountered them. This simple operation mechanically prescribed which threads would be woven into astonishingly elaborate designs. French silk weavers resisted the arrival of automation by throwing their wooden clogs, called *sabots*, into the works to halt production—and thereby engaged in history's first recorded acts of industrial sabotage. But resistance was futile. By 1812 there were 11,000 Jacquard looms at work in France alone, and the punched card was firmly established as a medium of input for machines.

BINARY ADDITION 101

$$0 + 0 \over 0$$

In binary, as in decimal, 0 + 0 = 0

$$0 + 1 \over 1$$

Similarly, in both systems 0 + 1 = 1

$$1 + 1 \over 1\ 0$$

But in binary, 1 + 1 necessitates a carry. Thus, 1 + 1 = 0, with 1 carried.

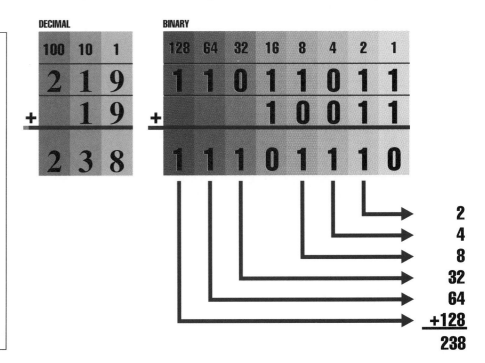

ADDING MORE NUMBERS

The two illustrations above show the same addition in both the decimal system and the binary. Both operate by adding the contents of successive columns, from right to left, moving carries when necessary. In the decimal version, 9 + 9 = 18. The 8 is written down, and the 1 is carried. In the binary version, 1 + 1 = 10. The 0 is written down, and the 1 is carried. The operation is repeated until the sum is complete. The arrows leading from the binary addition show a conversion of the sum back into the decimal system.

Its importance in data-processing was confirmed by the American inventor Herman Hollerith in his work for the U.S. Census Bureau. Hollerith designed an electro-mechanical tabulating machine to conduct the 1890 census; it used perforated cards for input. His tabulator was the only practical method of quickly compiling statistics on a population that had grown from 2.5 million in 1776 to more than 60 million. Operators sitting at consoles entered data on punched cards. They processed an average of 7,000 to 8,000 cards a day, and the record for a single operator was 19,071. The company founded by Hollerith eventually merged with others to become International Business Machines, or IBM. Punched cards and perforated paper survived as methods of data entry well into the 1970s.

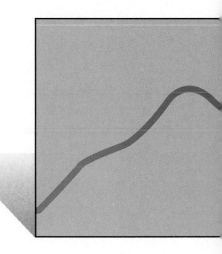

RUNNING THE GAMUT FROM A TO D

At the input stage, Hollerith's census tabulator was a digital, as opposed to analog, machine. Digital machines count or measure discrete entities, or separate events. A turnstile with a meter is a digital mechanism: it counts and records people passing through as discrete entities, one by one, as each person passes. Analog machines, by contrast, measure continuous, usually fluctuating values such as pressure, weight and temperature. An analog speedometer, for example, measures velocity as an ongoing phenomenon, not as a series of separate readings, and its needle rises and falls as a continuous display of miles or kilometers per hour. Electronic computers cannot process incoming analog data without first converting the signal into the crisp, digital units of its binary logic. The analog data enters the system through input devices called sensors, which work by modifying electrical currents to reflect changing conditions in whatever they are monitoring. The sensors express their measurements as a signal of fluctuating electric current.

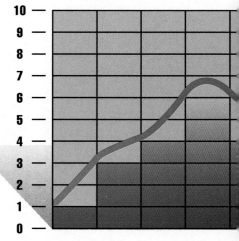

The analog-to-digital (A-to-D) converter, a microchip usually located in the input device itself, subjects the signal to periodic readings, called samples. Sampling is a rapid-fire process that "slices" analog information at regular intervals, and assigns a numerical value to each separate reading. The intervals between samples must be extremely fast to avoid a misleading conversion. A sampling rate of 20 to 30 times per second is typical for many sensors.

Information arrives at the computer in digital form. Whether it is data from a specialized analog sensor, or the digital signals sent from a general-purpose input device such as the keyboard, the information must be in the form of bits and bytes. These digital pulses of electricity enter the system through electronic gateways called ports, which come in two varieties, parallel and serial. Once inside the machine, data bits can only travel to the central processing unit—the CPU—in

FROM ANALOG TO DIGITAL

Computers cannot read analog information such as temperature readings or sound input, without first passing the data through an analog-to-digital converter.

1	3	4	6
0001	0011	0100	0110

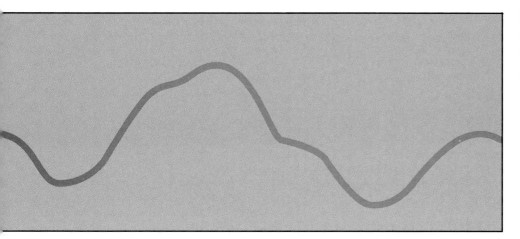

Raw input from such sources as sound and temperature readings is first converted into a continuously fluctuating analog signal.

To convert analog signals into digital form, the computer uses the technique of sampling—high speed readings that are taken at regular intervals.

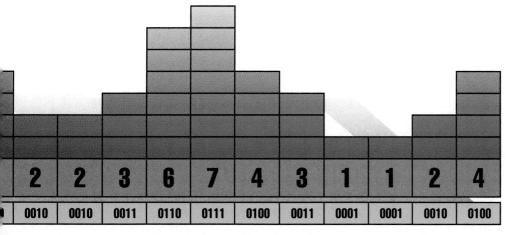

The last step in the conversion is to assign a binary numerical value to each of the readings. The input is now entirely digital.

2	2	3	6	7	4	3	1	1	2	4
0010	0010	0011	0110	0111	0100	0011	0001	0001	0010	0100

parallel groupings, alongside one another. Bits that are already arranged in parallel by an input device, enter simultaneously through a parallel port, and travel directly to the CPU. Bits that arrive serially, enter in single file through a serial port, as if through a turnstile. Once through, the serial port must then line them up in parallel before they can proceed to the CPU.

THE WORKHORSE OF INPUT

The basic layout of the keys on the computer keyboard evolved from an earlier office workhorse, the typewriter. First patented in 1867 by Christopher Latham Sholes, a Wisconsin newspaper editor and printer, the typewriter was successfully mass-marketed six years later by the firearms company E. Remington and Sons. That company went on to become Remington Rand, which in 1951 launched UNIVAC, the first commercial mainframe computer in the United States. Despite this distant kinship, however, the differences between computer keyboards and typewriters far outweigh their apparent similarities.

The first distinction is that the keys on a computer keyboard, unlike those of a typewriter, have no intrinsic meaning. The keys are marked with letters of the alphabet and numbers, but they can be assigned an infinite variety of other meanings, depending on what is wanted by program designers, systems engineers and even the individual user, who is also able to customize the keyboard. Thus, while depressing the letter Q means "Q" in a word-processing context, it can just as easily mean "Queen" in a chess program, or "Quit" in a math program. In some other application, it can be assigned a meaning that has no connection at all to the letter Q in the alphabet.

In addition to conventional typewriter keys, the keyboard also has function keys, which can be assigned a variety of tasks to meet the demands of different software packages. There are also several single-purpose keys on the keyboard. These include the cursor keys, which are used to move an on-screen marker called the cursor. The cursor's feedback helps the user interact with the computer by indicating the location of the next character to be entered.

Under the keyboard's surface is a circuit board with contacts and wires marking out a grid whose coordinates have a significance to the computer. Pressing any key closes a switch at an intersection on the matrix of wires printed on the circuit board. This generates a scan code, which identifies the key by a numerical set of coordinates. The scan code travels along a cable and through a keyboard port, directly to the CPU.

The CPU then consults a hard-wired electronic list called a look-up table, located in ROM—the computer's permanent, factory-installed Read Only Memory. The look-up table cross-references each scan code against a binary number that stands for a meaningful symbol, such as a letter of the alphabet. Typically, the look-up table defines keys according to the computer's usual functions: the entry of numerical data, for example, or the use of a particular alphabet for word-processing. Computers in Western countries usually convert scan codes into ASCII—American Standard Code for Information Interchange. This standard uses 128 binary numbers to represent upper- and lower-case letters, numerals, typographical symbols and a variety of codes that instruct the computer to perform such assorted functions as backspacing or sounding its beeper.

HANDS-ON INPUT

The keyboard is a fast, efficient device for entering text. Under the keyboard is a circuit board with a switch for each of the keys. Pressing a key is the first step of input.

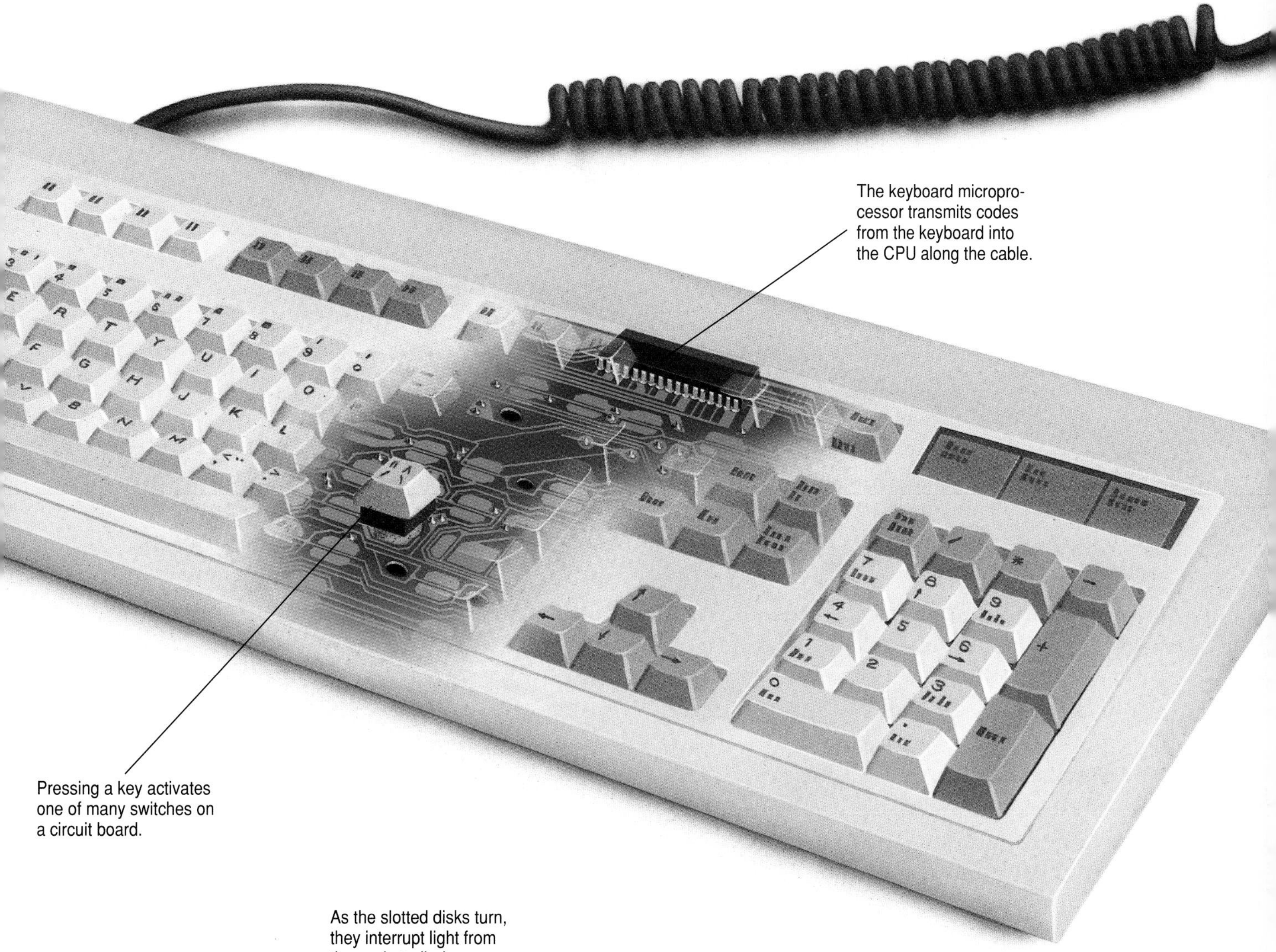

The keyboard micropro-
cessor transmits codes
from the keyboard into
the CPU along the cable.

Pressing a key activates
one of many switches on
a circuit board.

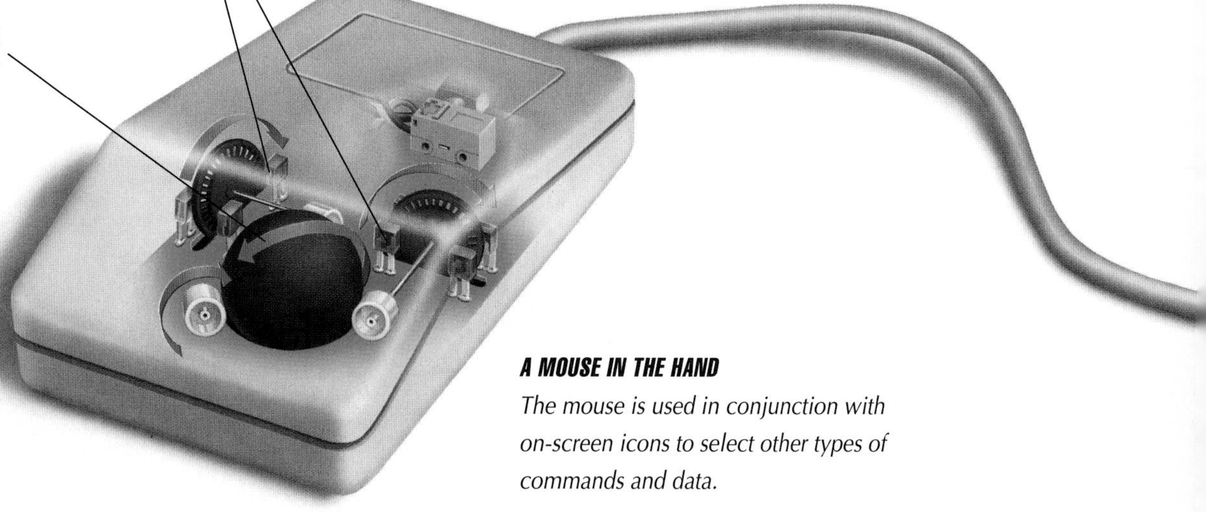

As the slotted disks turn,
they interrupt light from
these photodiodes.

The roller ball turns slotted
disks inside the mouse.

A MOUSE IN THE HAND

The mouse is used in conjunction with
on-screen icons to select other types of
commands and data.

MOUSE POWER

While the keyboard is a fast, efficient tool for entering text, the mouse is often far quicker and more convenient when it comes to moving the cursor around the screen. The mouse works as an analog for the cursor. Moving the mouse along a flat surface moves the cursor in the same relative direction on the screen. As the user propels the mouse along, his action changes the cursor's horizontal and vertical screen coordinates. By checking these "map references", the computer knows the position of the cursor. The software being used generates on-screen icons and menus tailored to each program. With the cursor positioned on the desired icon or menu, the user clicks function switches mounted on the mouse to send input into the computer. The mouse displays its advantage when it is used to point and click on icons and pull-down menus. It really comes into its own in graphic applications, when it is used as a paintbrush or a stylus, or to move graphics around the screen.

Mice come in two varieties, mechanical and optical. The more common mechanical mouse has several moving parts. The most conspicuous is a roller ball that is clearly visible underneath the device. As the mouse is guided by the user, the ball turns two slotted disks positioned at 90 degrees to each other. As they turn, they interrupt a beam of light produced by a light-emitting diode, or LED. Sensors called photodetectors register these pulses of light, and send slightly different signals to the computer, which enables it to determine the direction of movement. Apart from its function switches, there are no moving parts in an optical mouse. It can only work by passing over a special pad marked with a grid of vertical and horizontal lines. Light from the LEDs illuminates the surface of the pad, and a lens on the underside of the mouse focuses the image of the lines. The image is in turn reflected by a mirror onto a sensor called a photodetector. The information from the photodetector is translated into digital signals that the computer converts into

The joystick translates hand movement into a succession of screen coordinates, which results in the apparent movement of objects, often in games, on screen.

The musical instrument (left) looks a little like a flute and is, in fact, a wind instrument. Its controller (above), translates analog signals into digital form, permitting this one instrument to take on many voices, and enabling a single musician to sound like an orchestra.

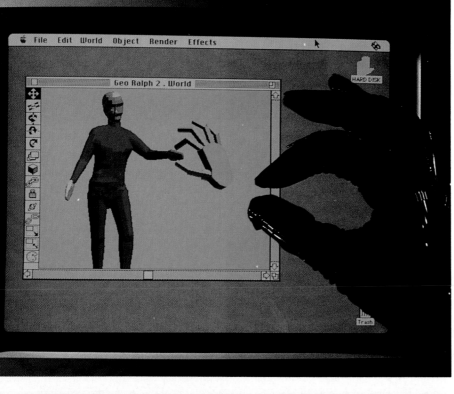

The bar code reader (above) *is an input device that scans the Universal Price Code lines printed on every package in a supermarket. The data is then routed by the store's computer to the cash register, to inventory control and even to distant suppliers for automatic re-ordering of stock.*

To reach out and touch a lifelike computer-generated world, the operator slips a data glove (top) snugly over his hand. Fiber optic cables looped on the back of the glove duplicate the movement of his fingers. As a result, light signals in the cables are interrupted; the interruptions send information to the computer. The user sees the visual display through special goggles (below) that complete the illusion of reality.

Easy Rider

Friday afternoon and it's rush hour in the city. Yet no tempers flare and car horns are noticeably silent. Such peace is possible because each car on the road is connected to an intelligent vehicle/highway system (IVHS). The cars carry computers that communicate directly with a control center through a network of infrared roadside beacons. Information streams into each car's onboard system at a rate of 8,000 digital characters per second and is used to tell the driver about road conditions, accidents ahead and the quickest way home. Many drivers simply sit back and monitor their display units; the cars are on autodrive.

This scenario is not a fantasy. Large experimental IVHS networks already exist in Europe and Japan. By the year 2000, many service and emergency vehicles may be connected to such electronic information systems. Domestic cars likely will become part of the network by 2020.

Computers are already playing a large role in automobiles. In fact, some cars have become four-wheeled information processors, receiving and analyzing input from both road and driver. Output comes instantly in the form of a mechanical response such as a smoother stop or an increase of fuel to the engine, or an electronic one such as a speedometer or compass reading on a heads-up windshield display.

The early 1970s oil crisis spurred electronic development in cars. New fuel injection systems improved gas economy and reduced emissions; electronic ignition timing ensured more reliable starts. Now the latest cars carry an array of sensors, located throughout the vehicle, that send information to nearby computers. They allow the car to react instantly to changing conditions.

In some models, if the car encounters rough roads a suspension computer responds by signaling a pump to send more oil to hydraulic shock absorbers. The smoother the road, the less oil is transferred to the shock absorbers, each of which adjusts individually to compensate for uneven loads. Electronic anti-lock brake systems prevent dangerous skids during sudden stops by automatically pumping the brakes 10 times faster than can a driver, and a computer guarantees that all four wheels brake evenly. Yet another computer constantly adjusts the engine so that it functions efficiently. Sensors in the engine monitor temperature, air intake, engine speed, and other vital information. Microchips are also used to control automatic transmissions and power steering.

In the future, even greater amounts of digital information will be stored at locations throughout cars. Through a system called multiplexing, data will be coordinated and efficiently moved through a single transmission line. New technology will be dedicated largely to navigation and collision avoidance systems. But motorists already are enjoying the benefits of electronic development as they drive cars that operate more cleanly, safely and efficiently than ever before.

TRAVELING COMPANIONS

Onboard, and usually invisible, computer technology is involved in many aspects of car performance, safety and entertainment. The hypothetical car at right contains electronic devices that are in use now, or will be by the turn of the century. The red components are the instrument and air control devices; the orange units are body electronics components including safety, security and the multiplexing system. Yellow modules are part of the audio and entertainment system and green ones control the car's steering and suspension. Integrated circuits and hybrid electronics, including braking devices and obstacle detectors, are indicated by blue, and the components which direct engine and powertrain electronics are violet.

Developed from jet-fighter technology, the Heads-Up Display *(top)* projects vehicle speed and other key information onto the windshield in the driver's field of vision. This allows drivers to view the information without taking their eyes off the road. Controls are provided to tailor display brightness and positioning on the windshield.

cursor movements on the screen. The trackball is simply an upside-down variant of the mouse. While a mouse must roam about a desktop or a pad to do its work, in a trackball only the roller ball moves. The unit itself remains stationary.

SPECIALIZED INPUT DEVICES

Keyboards and mice are the general practitioners of input, but many specialists have been devised. A number of them operate on the same principles as mice: They allow the user to select an on-screen cursor position from a grid of vertical and horizontal coordinates, and then to select and perform various functions by using onboard switches or buttons. This category includes the light pen, which is used to draw and erase directly on the screen. The digitizing tablet is another drawing device, often used in drafting. It consists of a rectangular pad that identifies the screen coordinates and acts as a radio transmitter, while its companion stylus acts as a receiver. The interactive touch-screen is a specially designed monitor that does double duty as both an input and an output device. At the surface of some touch-screens is a sandwich of two thin plastic sheets containing invisibly fine wires arranged in a matrix resembling a keyboard's circuit board. By responding to on-screen prompts, the user selects both the coordinates and the function switches directly, with the touch of a finger. This pressure is enough to make contact at specific intersection points on the matrix, and thus send commands and data into the computer for processing.

Optical scanning devices convert visual information such as photographs and printed text into a digital form that the computer can reproduce and send to the screen or other output devices, or to storage. The original image is illuminated, and its varying densities and colors are focused through a lens onto a sensing device. There, the image is divided into a grid of tiny boxes, resembling a mosaic. The box at each grid coordinate is assigned a numerical value, depending on the brightness and color it contains. The computer interprets all the numerical information it receives about the grid as a whole image.

Just as optical scanners assign numerical values to graphic images, sound digitizers turn audio input such as speech or music into numbers. Whatever the source of the sound, it must first be converted into an electrical signal—a standard method is to use a microphone, or a pickup on a musical instrument. The signal is sampled by a high speed, typically 44,000 times per second, A-to-D converter and rendered into bits and bytes. This technology is the driving force behind the astonishingly clear sounds that emanate from compact disk recordings. Compact disk technology is also used in computer storage methods using optical disk drives.

Automatic Teller Machines (ATMs), increasingly common in banking, are input devices that give the user access to a distant computer. They work in essentially the same way as a keyboard, with a grid of wires mounted behind the keypad. Even touch-tone telephones are input devices, since they too interact with computer systems. Each key on the phone generates an audible tone at a specific frequency. When the tones are converted into numerical values at the computerized telephone exchange, they instruct the system where to place the call. Personal computers can be equipped to convert the tones in applications such as home security systems—the user can phone instructions to various modules that control the lights, alarms and doors in the house.

HIDDEN TALENTS

The supermarket checkout bar code reader is an input device that hides many of its specialized talents. The raw input for the supermarket's computer is the merchandise on the shelves. Each package in the store is marked with a pattern of bars and spaces called the Universal Product Code. A wide bar or space signifies a one, and a thin bar or space indicates a zero. As the package passes over the reader, an internal laser generates a lattice of infrared beams that scans the bar code. The lines and spaces on the package interrupt the beams, and as they are reflected back into the mechanism, the scanner reads the interruptions as binary ones and zeros. The information is then processed by the supermarket's computer, and output is sent to a number of destinations. The output arrives at the cash register as an illuminated readout of the price on a display panel, as a printed receipt and sometimes also as a disembodied voice, mechanically checking off each item purchased. The data is also sent to the computer's inventory records. When stocks fall below a certain level on any given product, the computer automatically places orders for new supplies. The computer may even route the input from the bar code reader to a programmed marketing service that prints out price-reduction coupons, customized to the individual buying habits of each shopper. If the consumer buys several bottles of spaghetti sauce, for example, the coupon might be a special offer for a particular brand of Parmesan cheese.

Once at the exotic horizons of input, virtual reality devices such as data gloves, data suits and 3-D goggles are becoming part of the input mainstream. Such devices allow the user to experience the artificial reconstruction of a reality that is, for all practical purposes, indistinguishable from the real world—or from imaginary worlds for that matter. For example, virtual reality allows an architect to "walk through" perspective views of the interior of a building before it is constructed. A fighter pilot can now perceive, with all his senses, every adrenaline-pumping split second of an aerial dogfight—without leaving the ground. His every reaction to the simulated combat becomes part of the system's input. The decision to bank or climb, to fire or flee, is transmitted—through his handling of the controls—to the computer. The results of his decisions are fed back to him instantaneously. The instruments he sees, the sound effects he hears and the hydraulic mechanisms that move him so convincingly, are all part of his virtually real surroundings.

Input may be a deliberate, consciously willed step on the part of the user—for example the decision to select a certain command on a bank machine, or to delete a word from a block of text. It can just as easily be a hidden, invisible process as automatic devices sense such things as movement or temperature, and send data bits coursing into the CPU.

Input may be as varied as a word, a temperature reading, a brain scan, a photograph or the price of a pound of coffee, but to the computer it is all the same. The CPU makes no distinction between pictures, numbers and sounds. Although the process of input is seemingly instantaneous, a number of steps are involved. By the time the raw data has been entered and has passed through the input ports and the CPU into memory, it has all been transformed into binary numbers, the sole mathematical medium of exchange the CPU is capable of understanding and manipulating. Once the input has successfully entered the system, the stage is set for the computer's next vital step: processing.

Access to Input

The computer is a marvelous tool—provided the user can operate a keyboard, manipulate a mouse and see the screen. But for people with physical disabilities, working on standard machines can be an impossible task. Fortunately, there are a number of other ways to take advantage of a computer's potential.

Often the solutions are simple. Some people are able to use a head or mouth stick to tap information on a standard keyboard. In other cases, they use slightly modified equipment. An expanded keyboard, for example, has all the necessary elements: letters, function keys, cursor arrows. But it is large—a foot deep by two feet wide—and the keys are

hand-sized. A person who lacks fine muscle control may type on the keyboard with his fists or elbows. But the result is the same: input. People with even less motor function can operate a joystick-like mouse, mounted wherever it can be reached, with their lips, chin, shoulders or feet.

If a disabled person cannot manage a mouse, communication with the computer is still possible through simple switch and interface devices. The switch attaches to any part of the body and is turned on and off in various ways—with puffs of breath, tongue movements or controlled muscle contractions. It sends a series of signals to an interface device that translates them and sends

them on to the computer. For example, the user may systematically activate keys arrayed across a specially programmed electronic board, stopping at certain illuminated letter or symbol keys along the way. These keys, or combinations of them, send specific information to the computer.

Most visually impaired people can operate a standard keyboard, but they lack a means of double-checking their input until a braille printout is in their hands. A new braille system solves that problem. Near the keyboard is a translating device with a tactile display unit made up of small pistons that rise in braille patterns. The user reads the braille to check what is on screen.

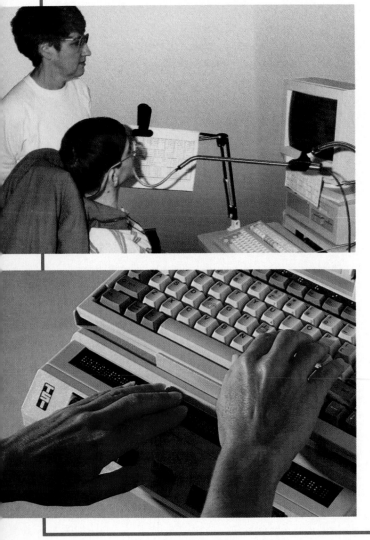

A single switch "sip and puff" device allows a disabled youngster (left) to enter input into a computer. He uses Morse code—a sip is a short dash, a puff is a long dash—to write a composition. The visually impaired can use a specialized braille system (below, left). A tactile display unit mounted below a standard keyboard uses patterns of tiny raised pistons to reflect the display on a computer video monitor in braille.

The child at right enters and retrieves information with a specialized computer communication aid. Despite her physical and speech impairments she sends complete sentences to her computer by pressing combinations of picture symbols on a large keyboard. The messages are then translated into synthesized human speech.

Voice input has long been the Holy Grail of this field. But until recently, computers that could recognize spoken words were either very expensive or had severely limited vocabularies. Now, a voice-activated program has been developed that recognizes 25,000 words and can be taught 5,000 more. The program adapts to a user's individual speech patterns and can differentiate between ordinary words and commands such as copy file or open dictionary.

Eventually some of these specialized devices—voice input, for example—will be universal. But the ultimate goal of technology is to make all computers equally accessible to everyone.

PROCESSING

With the power off and its monitor darkened, a computer is little more than a study in potential—and no more able to act on its own than any other electrical device deprived of electrons. But once its circuits have been animated by electricity, that potential is instantly transformed into an electronic power plant capable of processing reams of data at breakneck speeds, and generating equally prodigious reams of results with predictable accuracy. Indeed, given the opportunity to apply its data-crunching circuits to a single night's math homework—the homework of each and every elementary school student in the United States—even a humble personal computer would complete the job in about an hour, while a machine with a more powerful 32-bit microprocessor would sprint through the assignment in one, or at most two, minutes. A supercomputer would turn in the most impressive performance of all, whipping through billions of problems and turning in billions of correct answers in 10 seconds flat.

A supercomputer brings a vast amount of processing power to the job, and can handle hundreds of millions of individual calculations per second. It does so by first reducing them to such basic arithmetic and logic operations as simple addition, subtraction, multiplication, division and comparison. So, too, does the personal computer, whether it is being used to tap out term papers, balance the family budget or energize an evening's worth of computer games.

In each instance and in every computer, the coordinator behind the entire operation is the central processing unit, or CPU, which in most personal computers consists of a single silicon chip, or microprocessor. The CPU controls all the various parts of the computer, fetching and executing program instructions, shuttling data along electronic pathways called buses, and executing any arithmetic and logic operations required by the job at hand. Banks of memory bolster the computer's electronic processing power, while an internal clock acts as a kind of pacemaker, emitting electrical pulses that serve to synchronize the millions of decisions.

As trains are shunted through a switchyard, they must follow rigid rules under the watchful eye of a controller. Information travels through the computer's central processing unit in similar fashion—but at far greater speed.

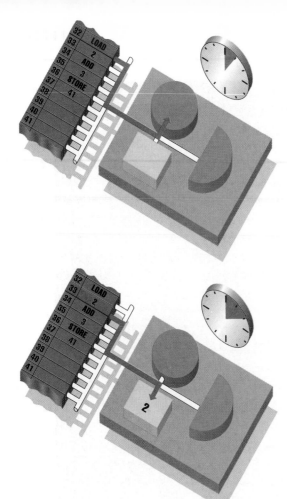

THE SIMPLEST ADDITION

To add two numbers—in this case 2+3—the computer takes a series of orderly steps, which are synchronized by its clock. At the first pulse of the clock, the control unit of the CPU fetches the program instruction LOAD from memory address 32. After decoding the instruction, the control unit knows it must now fetch the value 2 from the next memory address—33. The 2 is placed in a register.

CRUNCHING THE NUMBERS

With its every action governed by a fresh pulse from the clock, the control unit now retrieves the instruction ADD from memory address 34. That instruction is decoded in turn, and the control unit retrieves the value 3 from the next memory address, 35, and places it in the ALU. Next, the control unit copies the 2 in the register, and places it in the ALU. The ALU then adds the two values it holds—2+3. The result of the operation—5—is placed back in the register.

into the computer. In the case of a mathematical calculation, any instruction such as add or subtract is similarly translated into an instruction the CPU can understand.

The control unit of the CPU is served by a quartz crystal clock that generates pulses at a given frequency, measured in megahertz, and sets the pace for the flow of data and instructions. The clock can reside on the chip with the microprocessor, but more commonly it occupies a separate chip.

Processing of a calculation begins at the next pulse of the clock, which triggers the first of two complete instruction cycles, LOAD and ADD. Each cycle consists of four separate steps; during the first, the CPU fetches an instruction from memory. At each ensuing pulse of the clock, the CPU decodes the instruction, transfers needed data to one or more storage registers and finally performs the actual arithmetic operation.

Despite the number of individual steps involved in this one calculation, they all take place in a tiny fraction of a second, and the result appears on the monitor virtually at the instant of input. Such split-second timing is itself the direct result of the organizational skills of the CPU and its three main components: the control unit, temporary memory units called registers and the ALU. Typically, all three of these parts will make up a single microprocessor and will be found on the same chip.

As its name implies, the control unit of the CPU directs the various activities of the computer. Through its network of registers, decoders, counters and buses, it sequences, interprets and carries out the millions of instructions dictated by a particular software program.

As it goes about the business of following a program, the CPU is constantly ready to react to changing events such as the arrival of a new input from the keyboard. This type of event is called an interrupt. The CPU will momentarily give priority to any interrupt, and then automatically go back to the task at hand.

The CPU's tiny, high-speed memory banks, or registers, are each designed to hold a single data item or a single instruction as it enters and leaves the microprocessor. Among the various kinds of registers are instruction registers, which retain the program instructions; data registers, which hold items of information about to be processed; the program counter, which indicates the memory location of the next data item or instruction; and the accumulator, where the result of a particular calculation is held before being sent to its own memory location, prearranged by the program.

The third part of the CPU, the arithmetic logic unit, is responsible for the actual processing of data. Here, among many other operations, numbers are added, subtracted, multiplied and divided, and data is compared, all based on Boolean algebra and utilizing a system of electronic switches called logic gates.

Boolean algebra, developed by the 19th-Century British mathematician George Boole, is a system of thought that combines the symbols of algebra with the symbols of logic. In essence, Boole's system holds that logical propositions—statements that are either true or false—can be expressed as symbols. By employing any of

SUMMING UP

To be useful in any subsequent calculation, the result must be readily available at its own memory address, prearranged by the program—in this case, 41. The control unit retrieves the instruction STORE from memory address 36 and decodes it. The decoded instruction tells the control unit to fetch the value 41 from memory address 37. The result of the addition, the 5 held in the register, is then placed at memory address, 41.

A QUARTET OF PIONEERS

No one person can claim to have invented the computer in a flash of inspired insight. Hundreds of people have made theoretical and practical contributions to its development over several centuries. While the invention of the computer is a work in progress with no end in sight, it already owes a large debt to these four men.

During the 1930s, Konrad Zuse was working independently—and in some isolation—in Germany. He built two prototype calculator/computers, the Z1 and Z2, on the kitchen table of his father's home. His wartime Z3 and Z4 machines were functioning computers, used to solve engineering problems of aircraft and missile design. In 1942 he proposed redesigning the Z3, using vacuum tubes instead of electromechanical relays to control the flow of current. The computers he built featured the first use of binary input (on punched tape), a rudimentary central processing unit, a memory for storing numbers and an output unit. Zuse devised his own set of operating rules, and although he did not know it at the time, his rules were a practical application of Boolean logic. It took nearly two decades before computer historians accorded Zuse's homemade machines their rightful place in history as the first general purpose program-controlled computers.

Claude Shannon, a graduate student in his early 20s at the Massachusetts Institute of Technology, first made the essential connection between three key ideas: binary arithmetic; George Boole's system of algebra; and electrical circuits. All three of these elements were already well known, but it was Shannon who first realized that if electrical circuits which mimicked binary math were laid out according to the principles of Boolean algebra, they could then express logic and test the truth of propositions, as well as carry out complex calculations. His seminal 1938 master's thesis pointed the way toward the modern electronic digital computer.

On September 12, 1958 Jack Kilby *(left)* of Texas Instruments successfully tested the first primitive integrated circuit. Although his basic idea was a significant step, his design was somewhat rudimentary, and was quickly superseded by more elegant approaches devised by other companies. He shares the credit for the development of the IC with Robert Noyce *(right)*, one of the founders of Fairchild Semiconductors. Noyce contributed the idea of depositing thin strips of metal directly on the chip, eliminating the need for wiring, and his IC became the prototype for today's mass-produced chips.

several "logic operators" proposed by Boole—chiefly AND, OR and NOT—these symbols can then be compared and manipulated just as ordinary numbers can be compared and manipulated.

The similarity of Boole's two-state system of logic to the binary number system, while obvious today, was not so evident in the mid-1800s when Boole first published his theories. Decades would pass before later logicians, and the early American computer pioneer Claude Shannon, realized that Boole's system of true and false statements could represent the ones and zeros of the binary code, and the on and off states of an electrical circuit. Likewise, Boole's logic operators, updated as electrical switches, could become the cogs in a machine that would obligingly crank out the results of the most dizzyingly complex calculations. These adaptations of Boolean thought were synthesized by Shannon in his 1938 master's thesis at the Massachusetts Institute of Technology. The paper that laid the groundwork for the switching theory underlying modern telecommunications and computer technology turned George Boole—a self-taught mathematician and a university professor who never earned a degree—into an unwitting author of computer theory.

THE DICTATES OF LOGIC

Applied to a computer, Boolean algebra provided a precise, logical *modus operandi* for a machine designed to perform precisely and logically. Boole's logic operators now became logic gates, the most important of which—AND, OR and NOT—are the only ones needed to add, subtract, multiply and divide, or to compare symbols or numbers. Each gate—actually a microscopic switch fashioned from tiny transistors—controls the flow of electricity, and thus the flow of data and instructions, through a circuit. The ALU of the typical microprocessor contains thousands of these switches, wired together in various combinations to form logic circuits that allow the computer to perform both arithmetic and logic operations. Adders, for example, are logic circuits that do exactly what their name implies. Likewise, multipliers multiply.

Every logic gate is designed to accept one or more inputs in the form of binary numbers—either ones or zeros. The transistors making up the gate respond to these incoming signals according to the principles of Boolean algebra, and produce a single, predictable output—which will be also be expressed as a one or a zero.

To the computer, however, all those ones and zeros streaming through its circuits are actually pulses of electricity, of either high or low voltage, that open or close each logic gate. A high-voltage pulse, read by the gate as a binary one, will switch on a transistor within the gate and allow a separate pulse of current generated by the clock to pass to another gate, where it too will be read as a binary one. A low-voltage pulse, a binary zero to the gate, switches off the transistor in the gate and blocks the clock pulse. The next gate on that particular circuit will read a low-voltage current as a binary zero. The output of a logic gate also depends on the particular kind of gate and exactly what the inputs are. The logic gates are the bedrock foundation of all processing.

There are three basic types of logic gates. An AND gate requires two binary digits (bits) as input. The output of an AND gate is a one, if both inputs are one; otherwise the output is zero. An OR gate also admits two bits as input. The output of an OR gate is a zero if both inputs are zero; otherwise the output is one. A NOT gate takes only one input. The output of a NOT gate is the reverse of the input: if the input is a one, the output is a zero; if the input is a zero, the output is a one.

Other combinations of logic gates result in the creation of electronic circuits, such as adders and multipliers, that are tailored for specific tasks. One such device, the half adder, owes its name to the fact that it is used to add two binary digits, or bits, and thus just part of two binary numbers. Because it is unable to handle the third bit that a more complicated binary addition problem would entail, a half adder typically forms the first link in a chain of logic gates that ultimately does allow for more complex addition.

Half adders work by processing two bits of input, one from each number, and producing a single bit plus a carry, in accordance with the rules of binary arithmetic. The examples at far right demonstrate how a typical half adder would sum two different pairs of binary digits—in the first example generating a single total bit and no carry and in the second example a total bit plus a carry.

Carries pose a problem for half adders, however. For although a half adder can generate a carry, as in the second example, it can never receive one. Consequently, adding two binary numbers together, such as binary 11 and binary 10, is not as simple as linking the required number of half adders.

A better solution takes the form of a full adder *(page 61)*, a logic circuit that is capable of adding two bits and a carry. Connected to a half adder, a full adder takes the carry generated by the half adder, in this case 1, and adds it to the next

AND, OR, NOT—THE LOGIC GATES

All logic gates produce an output of one or zero. An AND gate needs two bits as input. It will deliver a one only if both inputs are one. Any other combination of inputs will produce a zero as output. An OR gate also requires two bits of input. It will produce a one if either or both of its inputs is one; it produces a zero only if both its inputs are zero. A NOT gate accepts just one input, which it then reverses, turning zeros into ones, and ones into zeros.

AND GATE

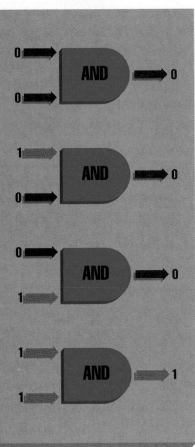

OR GATE

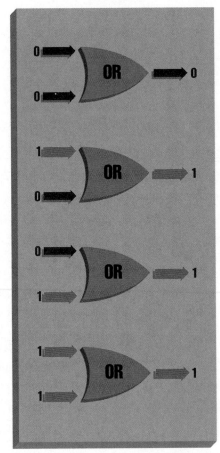

NOT GATE

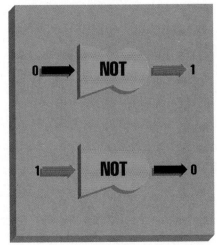

two input bits, two more 1s. The result, binary 110 or decimal 6, would spill from a computer's ALU as a sequence of two high- and one low-voltage impulses and be transferred to its accumulator.

But, of course, a computer would not be much of a computer if its powers were limited to the addition of simple two-bit numbers. Indeed, as it carries out its many roles, it often processes astronomically large figures. Accommodating larger numbers, however, requires larger logic circuits. Such devices consist of a series of adders—with one for each pair of bits—linked by OR gates and set up in such a way that the carries generated by one adder tumble, or cascade, into the next adder. In practice, this translates into a half adder to handle the first pair of bits in the problem, and, depending on the particular computer, as many as 63 full adders to handle the remaining pairs of bits, for a total of 64 bits. The resulting 64-bit microprocessor, with its extensive circuitry, is more likely to be found

HALF ADDERS

The circuit shown on this page is called a half adder. It is made up of AND, OR and NOT gates working in combination, each according to its prescribed response to input. A half adder can add two digits and produce a single digit result, (top). Or it can produce a two-digit result and pass on the carry, (bottom).

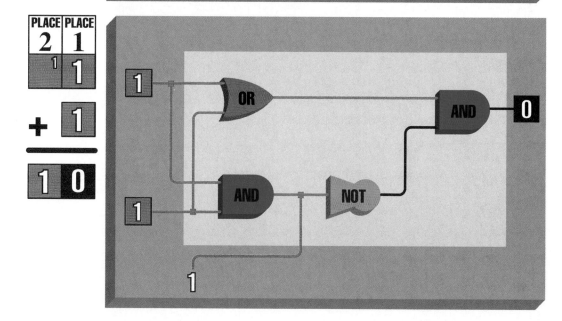

in supercomputers. Personal computers generally have been built around 8-bit or 16-bit microprocessors. Standards are changing constantly and the newer, more powerful desktop models are driven by 32-bit chips.

The circuit depicted on page 62 includes only four adders, specifically one half adder and three full adders. Such a circuit would permit the addition of two four-bit numbers, in this instance binary 0111 and 0110. As each adder does its job, the result is registered in the accumulator, while any carries drop into a lower adder. The whole process takes place at astonishing speed, and the result—in the form of electrical impulses—is almost immediately relayed to the accumulator.

THE RULES OF MEMORY

The same encoded pulses of electricity that allow computers to "think" also give the machine its remarkable ability to "remember," not only by means of the various registers incorporated into the CPU, but also through the computer's banks of internal memory, a key component of computing.

There are two kinds of internal memory: ROM, or read-only memory, and RAM, or random-access memory. Each takes the form of different types of microchips, and the typical computer will have at least one ROM chip and several RAM chips installed on its system board and linked to the CPU by buses.

ROM is the computer's long-term memory and is designed for the permanent storage of those instructions, including start-up programs, that allow the microprocessor to operate the computer. These instructions are programmed into ROM during manufacture and cannot be altered, or "written" to. They can, however, be "read" as often as needed by the CPU—a fact that accounts for the name "read-only memory." In addition, the information stored in ROM is "nonvolatile" and thus is not erased when power is shut off or lost. As a permanent, cast-in-silicon repository of essential information, ROM holds repeatedly used instructions which must always be available to any program in the machine.

By contrast, RAM is the computer's blackboard, a blank slate that can be written on, read from and then erased when the information is no longer needed. Accordingly, RAM is more correctly known as "read-and-write memory," even though this acronym actually stands for "random access memory," a term intended to indicate that any one byte of data is instantly accessible without having to search through the entire memory.

In its role as the computer's main working memory, RAM provides temporary storage for any program currently in use. It does the same for data needed for a particular operation, and for the results of processing. RAM is volatile, however, and is inherently subject to instant amnesia at the end of each work session. Everything in RAM is erased at the split second the power is shut off. As a result, programs and data too valuable to be entrusted to volatile memory must be stored externally on disks or tape. Programs and data installed in RAM are actually only copied into memory. The original remains on its storage disk or tape, safe from sudden power outages or data-devouring system errors.

Both RAM and ROM, like most other parts of the computer, have benefited from the trend toward miniaturization, as increasingly dense chips provide greater memory capacity. Back in the late 1970s, for example, a typical personal computer had 32 RAM chips which stored only 64K, or 65,536 bytes, of data—the equivalent

FULL ADDERS

The circuit shown at right is a full adder. Unlike a half adder, the full adder can accept a carry from a previous sum. In practice, the half adder is typically used to produce results that go into the first place column of an addition. The results generated by a full adder can go into any subsequent column. Like the half adder, the full adder can produce a single-digit result or a two-digit result with a carry.

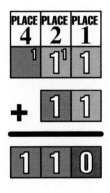

of an eight-page term paper. These days it is not uncommon for a single RAM chip to store 512K (the equivalent of 64 pages) and for the computer to have eight such chips. Access time—the split second it takes for the CPU to tap into the computer's memory—has also decreased, due to the infinitesimally short distances signals now have to travel during processing.

Although RAM chips differ from ROM chips in several significant ways, both are similarly composed of microscopic storage cells, the basic unit of semiconductor memory. Each cell can hold a single bit of information, and the typical RAM or ROM chip may contain thousands, or even millions, of such cells, each one so tiny that a quarter million of them could fit comfortably into the hole of a typewritten "o."

Access to those cells is controlled by transistors that switch on or off in response to high- or low-voltage signals transmitted by the CPU. The cells themselves are arranged in columns and rows, giving each cell distinctive horizontal and vertical coordinates that make it easy for the address decoder to select a particular cell at a particular memory location, or address.

In the case of ROM cells, the separate row and column decoders pinpoint the requested cell and then open it so that it can be read by the CPU. Although all ROM cells are capable of storing a charge, and thus a binary one, not all ROM cells will read as binary ones, since the gate transistors linking certain of the cells

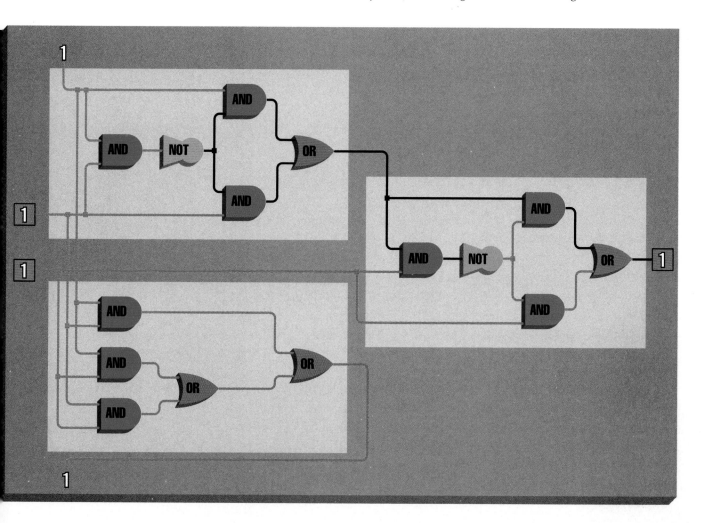

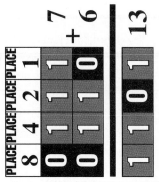

PLACE	PLACE	PLACE	PLACE		
8	**4**	**2**	**1**		
0	**1**	**1**	**1**		**7**
0	**1**	**1**	**0**	**+**	**6**
1	**1**	**0**	**1**		**13**

A CASCADE OF ADDERS

Half adders and full adders are linked into larger circuits to handle more complex calculations such as the binary addition—7 + 6—shown at right. The same problem is shown below and opposite, as it would be handled by such a circuit. The addition

requires a half adder for the first-place column, and a full adder for each successive column to the left. The half adder takes two inputs; full adders take three. Sums are sent to their column positions, while carries are passed from adder to adder as the third input.

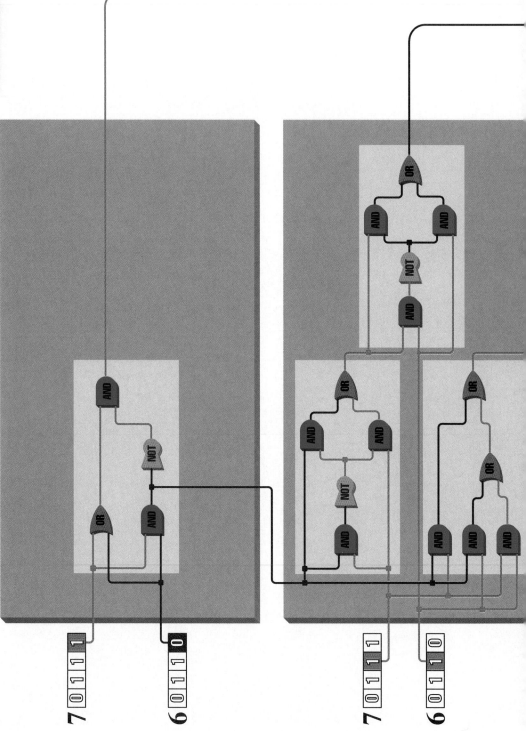

7 0 1 1 1

6 0 1 1 0

7 0 1 1 1

6 0 1 1 0

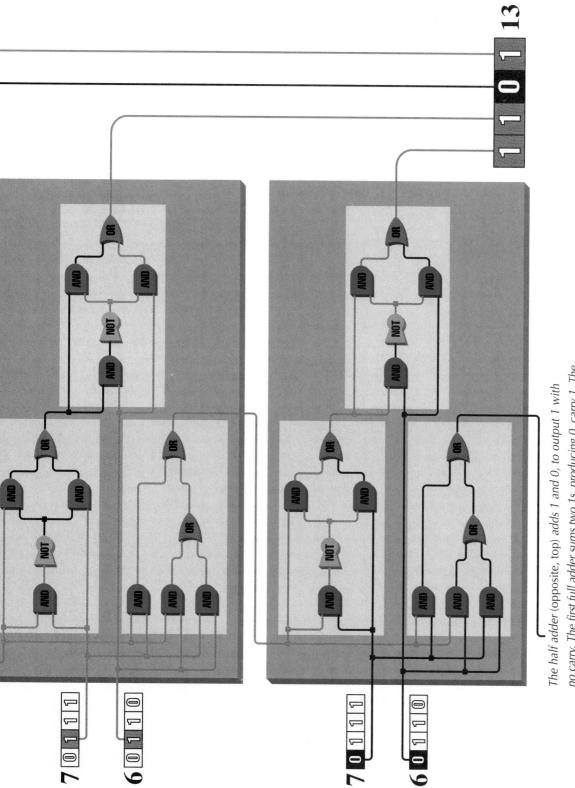

The half adder (opposite, top) adds 1 and 0, to output 1 with no carry. The first full adder sums two 1s, producing 0, carry 1. The next full adder adds two ones, and the previous adder's carry, to output 1, carry 1. The last full adder combines a pair of 0s and a carried 1, to output 1 with no carry. In each case where a carry is generated, it cascades to the next adder in the circuit.

Checkmate!

World chess champion Gary Kasparov fears no adversary—neither human, nor, for the time being, computer. In 1989 he took on the world's most powerful computer chess program, Deep Thought, confident of victory. While Kasparov pondered his strategy, Deep Thought examined two million possible board moves per second, sometimes anticipating 20 moves in advance. In just three minutes the program examined 360 million moves. Even so, Kasparov won both games convincingly.

Humans and chess programs approach the Game of Kings very differently. A grand master such as Gary Kasparov relies on learned strategies, his own powers of reasoning, plus a large measure of intuition and gamesmanship. A computer chess program, on the other hand, goes strictly by the numbers. It renders the rules of the game and the potential moves into numerical symbols and methodically acts upon rigidly defined logic operations. The program systematically searches and compares possible moves on the board until it reaches a decision.

To make a move, the program considers three primary criteria: which side has the most pieces, which has its pawns in the most advantageous position, and which has its King best protected.

It is mathematically possible for a computer to play absolutely unbeatable chess. But this would be very time-consuming—to say the least. To play a perfect game, the program would have to examine each of the estimated 10^{125} (10 followed by 124 zeros) lines of play that could follow from the opening position of the game. Even if it could examine one billion positions per second, (a rate about 1,000 times faster than Deep Thought), the computer would take 10^{108} years to complete the search for the first move.

In practice, a chess program carries out only a limited search. It employs a "brute force" approach to look ahead at all the possibilities to a depth of eight or 10 plies—a ply being one move by each side. At the same time, it examines certain crucial lines of play many plies deeper, using an algorithm named alpha-beta to weed out the less critical lines.

In addition to the search, many other considerations are taken into account—including the "contempt factor." This is an adjustable yardstick that tailors the program to respond to the differing skill levels in its human opponents. If the program is losing to a player considered before the contest by its programmers to be weaker—for whom it has contempt—it will continue to play aggressively, and try to win. However, the program will play for a draw if it falls behind an opponent with a higher pre-match evaluation.

Computer chess has developed quickly through programming advances and improved knowledge about how to represent the game to a computer. Hardware advances have played a part too—Deep Thought uses three computers, each with two large processing chips custom designed for chess. While absolute perfection will never be attained, the best chess programs have improved their International Chess Federation rating by a formidable 50 points every year since the 1970s. Should progress continue at this rate, Gary Kasparov may well be the last world champion to trounce a top-of-the-line program such as Deep Thought.

Two world chess champions face each other down. Gary Kasparov beat the world's best computer chess program, Deep Thought, twice in a two-game series in October, 1989. It took 53 moves to clinch the first victory, and 37 to thrash the program in game two.

to their column wires were permanently locked when the computer was programmed during manufacture. As a result of the severed connections, the CPU will be unable to detect charges in the selected cells and will interpret their absence as binary zeros. The charges in other ROM cells with their connections intact will be read as ones. Some ROM chips, called PROMs (for Programmable ROM), are designed to be programmed after manufacture. Once programmed, however, PROMs are forever programmed. Two other kinds, erasable PROM, or EPROM, and the electrically erasable PROM, or EEPROM, can be cleared and reprogrammed, either by a bath of ultraviolet light or by a burst of electricity of a specified voltage.

Row and column decoders are also used to locate memory cells in RAM. But RAM cells, unlike ROM cells, have microscopic capacitors wired to their gate transistors. These capacitors are designed to temporarily store an electrical charge, and since they can be activated and deactivated as often as necessary, they allow RAM to be written to, as well as read. To store data, for example, the address decoder activates a selected cell, momentarily switching on the cell's gate transistor and allowing current to flow into the capacitor. The transistor then switches off, trapping the charge in the capacitor. To read the data, the address decoder opens the gate transistor, releasing the charge, which will then be interpreted as a binary one; an empty capacitor will be read as a zero.

ROM AND RAM

ROM—Read Only Memory—is the computer's factory-installed set of instructions that is as unchanging as numbers carved in granite, whether the power is on or off. Its unalterable nature means that ROM can only hold instructions, but never store results. RAM—Random Access Memory—can be filled with information and erased as easily as a blackboard. RAM holds both instructions and results—but only so long as electricity powers its circuits.

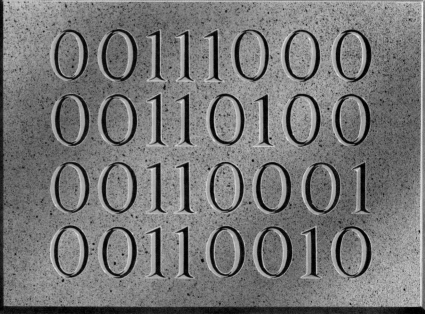

SERIAL PROBLEMS, PARALLEL SOLUTIONS

For all of their speed and efficiency, computers do have some problems inherent in their design. For example, charges stored in capacitors are short-lived, since electrons are able to leak into the surrounding silicon of the chip. Thus a charged capacitor will gradually lose its charge, even though its gate transistor is switched off. If enough of the charge is lost, the cell's contents could be mistaken for a binary zero by the CPU, with potentially chaotic results. To prevent this from happening, charged RAM memory cells are restored to vitality, or refreshed, by one of several circuits built into the chip—a process that takes place 500 times per second. RAM cells must also be recharged every time the cell is read, in order to ensure that the bit of data is retained in memory.

The need for recharging adds precious nanoseconds—billionths of a second—to RAM's access time. A microprocessor running at 8 MHz or 10 MHz would hardly notice such a minuscule delay. But newer, faster microprocessors—with speeds ranging from 16 MHz to 33 MHz—will find themselves waiting for data to arrive from memory. The resulting periods of downtime, or wait states, although measured in billionths of a second, can add up to a significant loss in processing speed. One way to sidestep such wait states is to forgo the dynamic RAM, or DRAM, commonly found in microcomputers for SRAM, or static RAM, which operates at faster speeds than DRAM and relies on pretzel-like circuits called flip-flops, rather than temperamental capacitors, to store data. Although SRAM is as volatile as DRAM and loses its memory if the computer loses its power, flip-flops will hold their charges without need for refreshing. This eliminates the problem of wait states associated with refreshing.

Wait states caused by slow memory can be avoided by installing a separate high-speed memory unit called a cache between the CPU and RAM. Much smaller and faster than DRAM, a cache anticipates operating instructions and needed data, and puts them at the disposal of the CPU. Since the cache is physically closer to the CPU and since data is more easily retrieved from a tiny cache than from the much larger main memory, access time is reduced and wait states are held to a minimum. Most of today's fastest microprocessors make use of some form of cached memory. Memory wait states are only one of several design drawbacks that can trigger a work slowdown in a computer. Ever-faster microprocessors, comparatively slower memory chips, increased traffic on buses, and the shortcomings of serial processing itself, all conspire to expose the limitations of von Neumann architecture. The problem is most apparent at the data bus, the electronic pathway linking the CPU to the computer's memory. Since the bus can only carry a single byte of data or one operating instruction at a time—and in only one direction at a time—the flow of data and instructions back and forth between the CPU and memory is restricted, and operating speed is slowed. The CPU of a conventional von Neumann machine thus has no alternative but to process a single instruction at a time. It also has no choice but to wait idly until the data bus is clear of data or instructions, at which point it reopens a path for the next byte. Faster microprocessors only compound the problem of too much traffic competing for the next available slot on the same single-lane highway, a problem that is called von Neumann's bottleneck. For some computer engineers, breaking the bottleneck has meant breaking with convention and redefining the configuration of von Neumann architecture.

Among the more successful of these innovations are memory caches, multiple buses and input/output processors that can direct electronic traffic to and from peripherals and memory, relieving the CPU of responsibility for printers and plotters that can run thousands or millions of times slower than the CPU itself. Another approach to breaking the bottleneck is to abandon serial processing altogether

Supercomputers: Flat-Out Speed

What does a black hole in space look like? What shape will airflow patterns take as they swirl over a jet aircraft flying at high altitude and hypersonic speeds?

It takes a supercomputer to make these invisible phenomena visible—and to take on a host of other problems that call for speed in processing. Supercomputers help engineers design spacecraft and automobile manufacturers design new cars; they allow medical researchers to trace the causes of aging disorders and moviemakers to create the most breathtaking special effects.

What makes a supercomputer "super" is its flat-out speed and its ability to take on calculations of immense complexity. To these ends, designers began by trying to pack as much power and speed as they could—the most efficient circuitry, the fastest switches—into single processor units. Most experts agree that the first modern supercomputer was the single processor CDC 6600, designed by engineer Seymour Cray for Control Data Corporation and introduced in 1964. After creating three powerful machines for Control Data, Cray went on to form his own company, Cray Research Inc. in 1972. Just four years later he unveiled the single processor Cray-1—complete with 60 miles of intricate wiring.

Single processor machines continue to provide fast and powerful processing today, but with the arrival of the Cray X-MP in 1982, supercomputers entered the world of parallel processing. Parallel processors link anywhere from two to eight processors to share the workload of a single computation.

Cray employee Steve Chen designed two multiple processor supercomputers, the Cray X-MP and Y-MP, which are still the workhorses of supercomputing. Chen left Cray in 1987 to found Supercomputer Systems Inc., and the two companies are locked in a race to complete ever-faster parallel processing machines. Within months Chen was building the SS-1, a 64-processor supercomputer that will operate on the outer edge of conventional parallel processing.

There is another, nonconventional, type of supercomputer that relies not on powerful circuitry but on advanced software to coordinate slower, more numerous processors. Called massively parallel, such processing machines link hundreds, thousands, and sometimes tens of thousands of processors together to tackle single problems.

The Connection Machine, completed in 1985, comprises an astounding 65,536 processors, each with its own memory. Inventor Daniel Hillis began designing it while he was still a graduate student at M.I.T. in the late 1970s. What he sought was nothing less than a supercomputer that would mimic the human brain. The Connection Machine's many processors are linked in a massive web; each processor is a node connected directly or indirectly to every other processor. With this design, the relationship between the processors can be reprogrammed to suit each task, in effect making the machine a newly configured computer that, like the brain, can approach different problems in different ways.

Supercomputers are already at work on problems that range from the creation of artificial intelligence to understanding the creation of the universe in the first explosive microseconds of its birth. As the diversity of new tasks increases, so will the need for ever-greater flexibility and power. There will never be a single, all-purpose, most powerful machine. Rather, there will be many different types of supercomputer to handle a growing multiplicity of assignments.

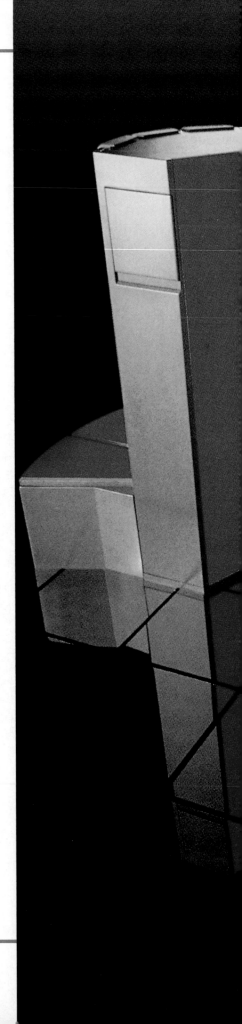

The distinctive supercomputer shown at right is a Cray Y-MP. It is currently one of the fastest, most powerful machines available. The Y-MP is used in applications ranging from automobile design to petroleum exploration, military research, biochemistry and weather forecasting.

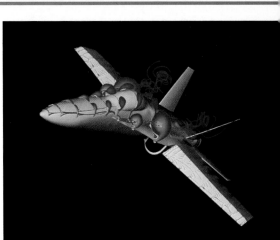

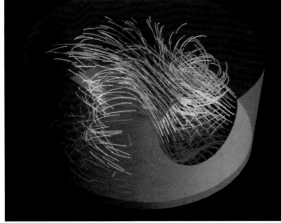

SUPERCOMPUTING AT WORK
These pictures show the supercomputer's calculation capacity to simulate the flow of a fluid over a solid object. The top two images show different views of the airflow over the surface of an F-18 aircraft. The bottom illustration is a simulation of the flow of blood through an artificial heart.

in favor of parallel processing. Unlike serial processing, in which one part of the computer works while the others take a breather, parallel processing spreads the workload by using many processors to solve a single problem.

The difference between the two kinds of processing is analogous to the contrast between the way a lone mechanic at the local garage works on a car and how a team of mechanics services a race car. The local mechanic works "serially," so that even the simplest maintenance—changing a car's oil, rotating the tires, replacing the spark plugs—is undertaken as a series of time-consuming steps. Race car mechanics, on the other hand, swarm over the car as it roars into a pit stop and perform multiple assignments in seconds, or at most minutes, merely by allocating a different task—or different parts of a task—to each member of the crew. At its simplest, parallel processing may involve the delegation of some of the CPU's authority by physically separating the control unit from the processor and then assigning various arithmetic or logic functions to specialized circuits within the processor. These dedicated circuits could then work on different parts of a given calculation, for example, at the same time. Separate instruction and data buses allow instructions to pass to and from the control unit and memory and data to flow back and forth from the processor to memory, thus reducing competition for the single bus found in many computers. A similar technique assigns a high-speed coprocessor—an electronic assistant—to the microprocessor. Typically, such a coprocessor would be responsible for arithmetic calculations, and only arithmetic calculations, relaying the results to the main processor.

Still another kind of parallelism, pipelining, transforms a computer's CPU into a processing assembly-line, allowing the machine to work on more than one instruction at a time. Ordinarily, on each pulse of a computer's clock, an instruction fetched from memory has to work its way sequentially through the various registers and decoders of the control unit before it can give the ALU its orders. Only then can the control unit fetch the next instruction and begin the entire instruction cycle over again. This process is inefficient since at any time during the cycle only one part of the CPU is working; the rest are idle. But in pipelining, the various elements of the control unit are organized as separate work stations that are able to work independently of each other. As a result, there can be as many instructions in the pipeline as there are work stations, with each instruction at a different stage of completion. As the clock pulses, the instructions move from work station to work station and finally activate the ALU. Even greater efficiency can be achieved by pipelining the ALU itself.

But even pipelining has been outstripped: nothing to date beats another kind of parallel computer, the processor array, which consists of multiple processors. Here, a single control unit is linked to the main memory and to every processor in the array, allowing the processors to communicate with one another. Each processor also has its own small local memory, which is loaded with data at the start of the program. The computer works by distributing the same instructions, one at a time, to each processor, which then carries out the instructions on data it retrieves from its own local memory. As a result, one processor completes its part of the job at the same time as the other processors are completing their parts. Nevertheless, having a single control unit limits a processor array to executing the same instructions simultaneously. To overcome that shortcoming, some computers give each

TEAM PLAYERS

The essence of parallel processing is the use of many processors to solve a single problem. The job is split into components and assigned to each of the CPUs, which work simultaneously to arrive at a solution.

processor its own control unit, producing multiple CPUs capable of carrying out different instructions—or entirely different programs—at the same time. One such computer, called a multiprocessor, features multiple control units linked to multiple processors, all connected to the same main memory. Another machine, the multicomputer, gives each CPU its own local memory, creating, in effect, a number of small computers within a computer. A large bank of main memory is accessible through a network that links each processing unit. Many of the hallmarks of parallel architecture have been incorporated into the design of the world's fastest and most powerful computers: the supercomputers. Capable of crunching numbers on a cosmic scale, supercomputers are being used in advanced weapons design and aerospace technology, among many other applications. In one of its more imaginative roles, a Cray supercomputer became the matchmaker in a computerized mating service for animals, taking just seconds to perform a job that had taken a less powerful microcomputer days: finding the ideal genetic matches for the zoo animals in its files. Such resourcefulness is as apparent in the design of supercomputers as it is in their application, and engineers are continually outdoing one another in a bid to build the most powerful machine. Toward that end, some new, trendsetting supercomputers combine tens of thousands of processors into massively parallel machines in an attempt to allow the processing of as many calculations at the same time. For all its speed and power, however, a supercomputer remains, like every computer, a prisoner of its program—the customized daily instructions given to the controller in the train yard. Without software, even so powerful a machine as a supercomputer is still nothing more than a machine. When it is properly programmed, however, any computer of any size becomes at once the master of its own switchyard.

FOLLOWING INSTRUCTIONS

Software. The word sounds compliant, even friendly, conveying the impression that at least one aspect of computing might make allowances for human frailties. Yet the programs that give the computer its multiple personalities and make it such a flexible tool are every bit as uncompromising as the electronic circuitry they control.

Software falls into a few general categories. The most basic is a collection of programs known as the operating system, a behind-the-scenes worker that performs routine housekeeping for the computer. The operating system coordinates the machine's activities, allocating its hardware resources and managing data handling and storage. In addition, it controls the machine's input and output, a function that also enables it to act as mediator between the computer and the user. To this end, some operating systems create a user interface—a simplified means of communication that, in effect, allows the computer to explain its actions and gives the user easy ways to tell it what to do next.

While the operating system takes care of these technical chores, applications programs—ranging from flight simulators and word processors to typing tutors and chess masters—concentrate on applying the computer's power to the task at hand. Finally, programs called translators allow the user to employ high-level computer languages for one of the most arduous tasks of all: creating new software.

Writing software requires the utmost precision. The list of instructions that make up a program must prescribe the computer's action in every situation that could conceivably arise in the course of the job the program was designed to do. For example, a simple program directing the computer to accept a letter typed at a keyboard and display it on a monitor might be expressed as BEGIN; READ ONE-KEY FROM KEYBOARD; WRITE ONE-KEY TO SCREEN; END. To display a series of characters on screen, however, would mean adding an instruction called a loop to repeat the read-write sequence. Clearly, even the most rudimentary word processing program would have many layers of such instructions.

A program, like an orchestral score, is a detailed, exacting list of instructions. It must be precise and without ambiguity. But while musicians may improvise, adding their own flourishes and interpretations, the computer cannot deviate from the program.

Although this sample program is written in a form resembling natural human language, computer programs are vastly different from human conversation in one critical respect: From beginning to end, they must be utterly logical and precise. Unlike a human, a computer can do only what it is told. It cannot infer meaning from a vague directive and act on what it thinks the user meant. In the worst instances, ambiguity could cause the computer to shut down altogether, with a possible loss of data. Consequently, programs must be carefully composed, using sequences of symbols that are strictly defined to mean exactly the same thing every time they appear. Those definitions are codified in the rules of computer languages, which are used to write all software.

LEVELS OF LANGUAGE

Just as human languages have distinctive rules of grammar and syntax, each computer language has a unique set of rules governing the way words, letters and numerals are used to communicate with the computer. High-level computer languages, which look like rough approximations of human discourse, enable users to create programs for a multitude of purposes, from number-crunching to writing music. No one language is perfectly suited to every situation, however. Some may have sophisticated abilities to handle graphics; others may be better at generating sounds or manipulating scientific formulas.

Usually, a programmer chooses a particular language not only because it is appropriate to the problem to be solved, but also because it is easy to use. But no matter how well a high-level language works for its human users, any program written in that language must ultimately communicate to the computer in the zeros and ones of machine code, a small set of binary instructions (about 200 in a modern computer) unique to each type of computer. During the 1940s, the earliest programmers wrote software directly in machine code, stringing together different sequences of zeros and ones that represented not only the instructions, but also the data to be manipulated and the numbered locations within memory where data was to be stored. Machine-code programming was an excruciating, error-ridden task, and before long computer users were looking for relief.

The solution was to write programs in terms that humans could understand, then to use the computer to translate them into its own machine code. By the early 1950s, some computers were equipped with simple systems that used short mnemonic symbols—letters, numbers, short words such as ADD and WRITE—to represent each of the machine instructions. The symbols were converted into the binary sequences of machine code by translator programs called assemblers, which could also keep track of memory locations, relieving programmers of this tedious

1 Get out at exit 61. Turn right at the first intersection.

2 Cross the railroad tracks, take the right fork at the big tree.

3 Turn left at the gas station.

4 Keep going until you see the church, turn right and drive for two miles. Turn left at the driveway.

ONE STEP AT A TIME

A program is arranged in steps, like the directions that accompany this map. In order for the steps to make any sense, they must be followed in sequence.

job. After the assembler produced the machine code program—usually on punched cards or paper tape—the user could feed the program back into the computer whenever it was needed.

Assembly language, as this kind of programming tool came to be known, is far closer to machine code than to natural language, and is difficult to learn and use. Programmers must be intimately acquainted with the computer's processes, and remember the many steps required for every task, even one as simple as adding two numbers. Because each assembly language works only on the type of computer it was designed for, a program written in one machine's assembly language is meaningless to a different kind of computer. Nevertheless, some programmers still employ assembly language. Its close correspondence with machine code makes it well suited for writing programs that require the fast, efficient use of a computer's resources. But for most applications, the drawbacks of assembly language outweigh its advantages. With the emergence of high-level languages in the late 1950s, assembly language became mostly a specialist's tool.

Like assembly language, a high-level language allows programmers to work with symbols rather than binary code. However, each symbol of a high-level language usually corresponds to a whole sequence of machine instructions. A high-level PRINT command, for instance, might initiate scores of machine operations resulting in a piece of data being sent to the printer. This feature not only puts more power at the programmer's disposal, it also reduces the need to understand specific machine operations. Furthermore, because a high-level language usually bears at least a passing resemblance to natural language, it is easier to learn, and programs are more readily understood by people other than the original programmers. Despite the enormous human advantages of programming in high-level languages, however, the computer itself is intractably monolingual. It understands only the limited set of zeros and ones of its own machine code, and needs special programs called interpreters and compilers to translate.

An interpreter works like a simultaneous translator, reading the written program (known as source code) one section at a time. It translates that section into binary instructions (or object code), then tells the computer to execute the new piece of object code. It works its way through the program piece by piece, translating, executing and discarding object code until it comes to the end. Because the source code is the only permanent part of the process, the interpreter must be in the computer each time the program is run. This side-by-side operation allows users to modify their source code on the fly and see the outcome immediately, but it also results in relatively slow program execution. In the quest for a more effective translator, language designers began in the early 1950s to develop a new type of program called a compiler. Instead of breaking the program into pieces, a compiler translates the entire body of source code into a complete object code program. Once the program is translated, or compiled, the compiler is no longer necessary; the object code program can be used independently at any time.

The first successful compiler, for a scientific language called FORTRAN (Formula Translator), took more than three years to develop. John Backus, an IBM programmer who headed the effort, found that developing the structure of the language itself—making it at once easy to use and sufficiently powerful—was the least of his problems. Far more difficult obstacles arose in writing the compiler program, which had to be capable of producing object code as efficient as that written by a human programmer, and doing it in such a way that it would not consume too much computer time, which in those days was far more precious than "people time." When it was completed, the compiler ran to 25,000 lines of machine code, which could translate just 32 high-level commands.

The version of the compiler that was distributed to users in 1957 had enough minor defects, or bugs, to discourage some users. But as the bugs were ironed out, FORTRAN began to show its strengths. After mastering FORTRAN's simple repertoire of commands, the user could write source code for all manner of programs, leaving the rest of the work to the compiler, which produced efficient machine code. Furthermore, because FORTRAN compilers were soon available for many kinds of computers, programmers no longer needed to learn a different language for every machine. A FORTRAN program written for one computer could usually run on another with only minor modifications—an economy impossible with machine code or assembly language programs.

Because it had been designed for scientists and engineers, FORTRAN was ill-suited to most other applications. New compiled languages quickly filled the gaps, however. Some were special-purpose languages such as APT (Automatically Programmed Tools), used to control the milling machines that shape metal parts for aircraft and automobiles. Others were more general in scope. For example, COBOL (Common Business Oriented Language) was a data-processing language that appeared in 1960, and BASIC (Beginners All-purpose Symbolic Instruction Code) was widely used to teach programming during the 1960s and 1970s, and continues in wide use today. All helped to broaden access to computers by making them easier to program. Even amateurs working with personal computers could create impressive software, and the programs produced and marketed by professionals became ever more powerful and elaborate.

Freed by high-level languages from slavish attention to the inner workings of a computer, programmers could increasingly shape their work to follow the contours of a problem. But if they no longer had to worry about remembering cryptic symbols and memory addresses, programmers were (and are) still bound by the rigidity inherent in the languages themselves. The form of every program is governed by the strict dictates of the syntax, or grammar rules, of the particular lan-

LANGUAGES

Computer programmers need to know several languages because there is no single, multipurpose language to meet all their needs. Each is suited to a specific type of problem and designed for maximum efficiency in its prescribed task.

Because early computers were used primarily for science and engineering, one of the first languages was FORTRAN, a specialist in mathematical calculation. But potential business users of computers had a very different set of requirements. The answer was COBOL, a language that enabled business to organize and update information in filing systems that resembled common business practices.

Both COBOL and FORTRAN required intensive study before they could be used, but BASIC was developed for more general programmers. No special knowledge of computers or mathematics is needed to program in BASIC, and it comes "bundled" with most personal computers as part of the software package.

The new wave in programming languages is the "metaphor-based" system, best exemplified by Apple Computer's HyperCard. A HyperCard program is considered as a set of index cards called a stack, with each card pointing to another, elsewhere in the stack. A card may play a tune or show a short piece of animation, a still image, or text. A complete application is set up by linking many cards in a sequence.

```
PRINT-AMOUNT-ON CHECK
        MOVE EMPLOYEE-AMOUNT-TO-BE-PAID
            TO CHECK-DOLLAR-AND-CENTS-
AMOUNT
        MOVE EMPLOYEE-AMOUNT-TO-BE-PAID
            TO WORK-TOTAL-AMOUNT
        MOVE WORK-DOLLAR-AMOUNT
            TO CHECK-DOLLAR-AMOUNT
```

COBOL (Common Business Oriented Language) is still the most widely used language for business applications on large and mid-sized computer systems. Its vocabulary mimics common business functions.

```
VAR
    message : STRING
BEGIN
    message : = " I think
    therefore I am. " ;
    write 1 n(message);
END
```

Pascal is named for Blaise Pascal, the French mathematician and inventor. Originally designed for teaching programming, Pascal is now widely used to write business and scientific programs.

```
* (DE CELSIUS (X) (*QUO( − x32)
1.8)
    CELSIUS
*(EVAL / (CELSIUS 104)
    40.0
*
```

LISP (List Processing) is a language primarily designed to process data that consists of lists. It is especially suited for text manipulation and analysis.

```
10   INPUT "What is your name ?" ; N$
20   PRINT "Hello," ; N$
30   END
```

BASIC (Beginners All-purpose Symbolic Instruction Code) enables non-programmers to write simple programs. It is usually included with personal computers.

```
    SUM  0.0
C Compute the average of a set of values
    DO 100 1 = 1, LAST
100   SUM = SUM + A (1)
    AVER = SUM /LAST
```

FORTRAN (Formula Translator) is used to write programs for engineering and a range of scientific applications. Its strength lies in its handling of mathematical formulas.

```
on mouseUp
    if field "guess" is in field "answer"
        then show field "answer"
    else
        beep
        answer "Sorry. Try again"
    end if
end mouseUp
```

Metaphor-based languages such as **HyperCard** organize information into what appears on screen as stacks of index cards, which the user can then manipulate to create applications.

RESTATE THE PROBLEM

1

The first step in writing a program is to restate any problem as a list of events leading to a solution.

WRITE FLOWCHART

2

The next step is to write a flowchart—a graphic representation of the sequence of events.

HOW TO WRITE A PROGRAM

This diagram shows a simplified rendition of the way a program is written. Just as programs are made up of lists of instructions, the business of writing programs involves a logical sequence of steps.

WRITE CODE

3

The flowchart must now be translated into the computer language chosen for the task.

TEST

4

Once the program has been written it is put through its paces in test runs.

DOES IT WORK?

5

YES

An evaluation is then made of the test runs. Careful note is made of any problems.

guage, which dictates the ways that the program elements can be combined.

The first step in writing a program, though, has little to do with the language. Instead, the programmer must arrive at a clear and unambiguous definition of the problem that the program is intended to solve. In some cases, this may require designing the task itself—specifying the objective and then breaking the work down into the procedures required to achieve it. The larger the job, the more difficult this aspect becomes, requiring the programmer to divide the job into segments small enough for one person to comprehend in their entirety. The relations between these segments, of course, also must be clearly stated.

DRAWING A DIAGRAM

When the theoretical analysis of the problem is complete, the programmer can design a step-by-step plan, or algorithm, for solving it. The algorithm can be stated in natural language. It is simply a complete, logical expression of the computational methods that lead to the solution. Some programmers use conceptual diagrams called flowcharts, to help organize their problem-thinking. Flowcharts employ standardized symbols to represent the various steps of an algorithm, and serve as maps for its complex pathways of logic. They are particularly useful for large projects, when several programmers may be working on different sections of the job. Flowcharts provide visual indications of the place that each part will take in the finished product. Many organizations, in fact, require that programmers provide flowcharts for all their work.

With a complete algorithm in hand, the programmer can proceed to the job of actually writing code, translating the steps of the logical process into the precise instructions of the computer language. This part of the task requires extreme care, since the least violation of the language's syntax can introduce a flaw called a bug that will keep the program from running or compiling properly. Compilers are designed to check for such errors and report them to the programmer, who can change the source code accordingly. More deep-seated errors in logic or conception, however, are harder to catch, and are the subject of the next phase of programming, known as debugging.

The trial-and-error process of debugging consumes as much as half the time required to produce a new program. First, the program, or a segment of a large program, is loaded into the computer and run until an error manifests itself by making the program behave mysteriously, or stopping it altogether. The programmer must then trace the bug to its origin, correct the source code, re-compile the program and run it again, repeating the steps until no more errors appear. New bugs may arise from debugging changes, and others may appear only when segments written independently are combined into the final program. Some of the subtlest bugs have no catastrophic effect on the program, but must be eliminated because they make it unacceptably slow, complex or unpredictable. Debugging often continues long after the nominal completion of software, as users put programs through paces designers never thought of, often discovering new bugs.

The final step in preparing software is writing documentation for users and other programmers. These instruction manuals and tutorials are essential to help the user master the software system. Documentation materials should clearly present the program in terms similar to those used in the initial analysis of the problem, showing users how to fit the problem into the software and then run the program to produce the desired results.

READING, WRITING—IN ARITHMETIC

Although the programming process is similar for virtually every kind of software, the resulting programs can be enormously different, both in the algorithms that describe them and in the ways they control the computer. For example, adroit memory management is the very essence of word processing software, the most popular application for personal computers. These programs can operate on documents as short and simple as a memo or as long and complex as a book filled with mathematical equations and different kinds of type. Word processors do their work by juggling words with lightning speed—moving, copying, deleting, formatting, printing and even checking them for spelling and grammatical errors at the user's command. But where an editor working with words on paper would have to use scissors and paste to physically rearrange the text, word processing software simply changes the order in which it retrieves words from memory.

The program sets up a part of the computer's main memory as a place for the sequential storage of text elements—letters, numbers, punctuation marks and spaces. In addition to this document memory, the program establishes a working memory area for temporary storage of text that is being moved or copied to another

If the program performs properly, the last step is to write the documentation, or user's manual.

If the evaluation uncovers problems in the program, debugging corrections are made and the program is sent back for testing.

part of the document. The program also uses part of working memory as a sort of address book. Memory slots at certain fixed locations hold details about the current positions of various data elements that may move around the document. The slots in working memory, called pointers, may keep track of such locations in document memory as the end of text, or the current position of the cursor. Thus, when the user wants to insert new copy in the middle of a document, or move a piece of text, the text already stored in memory does not need to be altered. Instead, the new material is simply appended to the end of the paragraph or document. When the user saves the document to a disk, the program rearranges the segments to put them in their proper order.

Electronic cut-and-paste is only the beginning of modern word processing's bag of tricks. The programs can also perform feats of formatting, modifying such properties as column width, line spacing, page length and typeface. Each of these specialties is governed by control codes stored in memory but not directly displayed—only the effects of the codes show on the screen. When the program encounters the control code for an underlined word, for example, it sends the letters of the word to the operating system along with the instruction to begin underlining. The operating system, which appends a special data packet called an attribute byte to each character it sends to the screen, alters the attribute bytes, telling the monitor to display underlined characters. When the program countermands the instruction, the operating system switches the attribute bytes back to normal type.

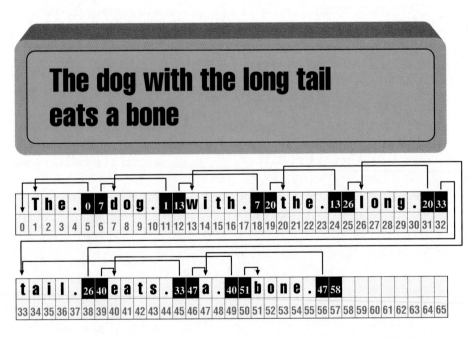

WORD PROCESSING

Word processing software gives users enormous flexibility in editing text. Such programs enable writers to add, delete or move text—word by word, or in entire blocks. The software can change the appearance of words by using different fonts, or type styles, as well as by underlining, bolding and formatting the text on the screen. Built-in dictionaries and thesauruses add to the software's versatility.

The upper part of the illustration shows a sentence as it appears on screen; the lower portion shows its organization in the computer's memory (the numbers on the bottom row represent the numerical address of each letter or space on the screen). Word processing software manages text with a linked list of units. In this example, each unit is a word, consisting of letters and numerical "pointers" that show the order of the text. The word **dog**, *for example, is followed by the pointers 1 and 13. The 1 points to the previous word, and the 13 points to the following word.*

When the user inserts the word **brown**, it is displayed on screen in the desired position, in front of the word **dog**. In memory, however, the new word is placed at the end of the sentence, and the pointers on either side of the word **dog** are adjusted.

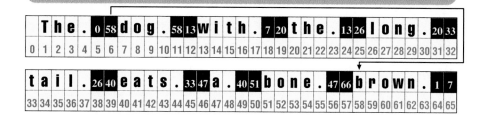

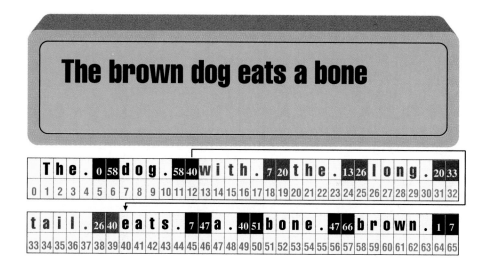

If the user deletes a block of text—in this example, the words **with the long tail**—the program adjusts the pointers so that the word **dog** now points to the word **eats**.

As the user enters, moves or deletes text, the change is immediately displayed in the correct order on screen, but not in memory. The program rearranges the text in memory later, putting it into the correct order during pauses in the work session.

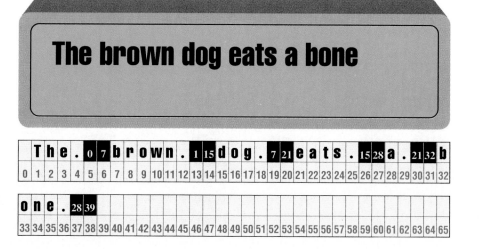

CALCULATING BOX SCORES

Another popular kind of software called a spreadsheet excels by taking advantage of the computer's innate number-crunching ability. Spreadsheets have taken over much of the repetitive drudgery of keeping business accounts. They allow users to write budgets, manage inventories, and analyze financial information. Spreadsheets offer control over the welter of numerical data and mathematical calculations that are an inevitable fact of life for businesses of all sizes. The spreadsheet's most useful feature is its talent as a tool for making informed predictions. It gives a business the ability to forecast accurately and rapidly the outcome of thousands of "what-if" scenarios. The effects of projected sales increases, or of any changes in the costs of doing business, can all be seen in an instant, as a ripple effect that washes through the entire pool of numbers.

On the computer screen, a spreadsheet looks much like the bookkeepers' ledgers it replaces. A grid of cells covers the screen. Each cell is identified by column and row in an arrangement resembling the latitude and longitude coordinates on a map. The user prepares the spreadsheet for use by assigning identifying labels to the columns. The labels can stand for anything the user chooses. A typical exam-

THE SPREADSHEET AT WORK

Spreadsheets analyze information arranged in tables. Such software makes it possible to see the global effect of changing a single numerical value in a table.

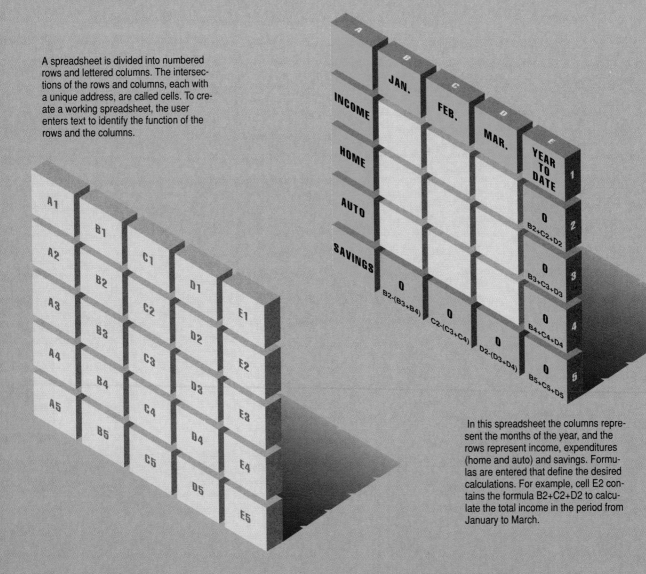

A spreadsheet is divided into numbered rows and lettered columns. The intersections of the rows and columns, each with a unique address, are called cells. To create a working spreadsheet, the user enters text to identify the function of the rows and the columns.

In this spreadsheet the columns represent the months of the year, and the rows represent income, expenditures (home and auto) and savings. Formulas are entered that define the desired calculations. For example, cell E2 contains the formula B2+C2+D2 to calculate the total income in the period from January to March.

ple could be a monthly sales breakdown, with one month assigned to each column. The next step is to assign algebraic formulas for various calculations to a row or column of cells. The formulas refer only to the coordinates—the map references—of the cells involved, not to their specific contents at any given time. For example, the formula A1 + A2 adds the contents of these two cells.

The user now enters numerical values into the appropriate cells—actual sales or expense figures for example—and instructs the spreadsheet to make a specific calculation by invoking a formula. The computer then fetches the contents of the cells involved, performs the specified computation, and displays the result. To try out a "what-if?" scenario, the user simply inserts new data into a given cell, and sees its consequences in other parts of the spreadsheet, without changing any previously established routines. A corporate planner, for example, can translate the company's entire financial structure into formulas in a spreadsheet. Then, to test the effect on profits of changes in such factors as wages or costs for raw materials, the planner puts new values into the appropriate cells. Without a spreadsheet program, each test of this kind would require laborious hand calculations through the entire sheet, with all the attendant potential for error. The software, however,

Once the spreadsheet has been set up, actual values can be entered. As this information is entered, the formulas automatically calculate the results. In this example income totals 7000, and savings total 2450.

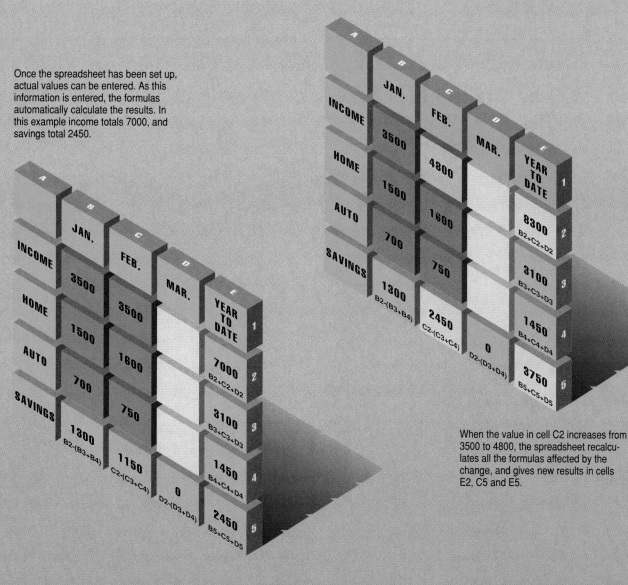

When the value in cell C2 increases from 3500 to 4800, the spreadsheet recalculates all the formulas affected by the change, and gives new results in cells E2, C5 and E5.

takes care of this computing and recomputing in a flash, changing the results of each affected formula, all the way to the bottom line.

A spreadsheet would be of little use if its capacity were limited by the size of an ordinary computer monitor, which can display only a few dozen cells at a time. The huge volumes of numbers required by many business applications may fill hundreds of columns and thousands of rows. With simple commands or keystrokes the user can get from one part of the sheet to another. The program performs tricks of memory to make the screen into a kind of moving window that swoops across the entire field of numbers and stops over any selected region.

A modern spreadsheet program has scores of built-in functions that go far beyond simple arithmetic. Some are specific to business use, allowing addition and subtraction of dates or one-step calculations of compound interest. Other commands adapt the software for scientific calculations that require frequent use of trigonometric and logarithmic functions. Furthermore, the program has facilities for treating numbers differently in various applications, using currency signs and two-place decimals for financial calculations, or many decimal places and exponential notation as necessary for scientific work. And when the number-crunching is done, most programs can turn the results into charts and graphs that help communicate the information at a glance.

DATABASE—THE VERSATILE FILING SYSTEM

Virtually every organization, from social club to multinational corporation, relies on record-keeping to stay organized, and computers are particularly adept at data-handling chores. Their electronic searching abilities make short work of the limitations inherent in even the most sophisticated filing systems. A mail-order retailer, for instance, might keep a list of customers on index cards, in alphabetical order. Although this arrangement would make it easy to find information about any individual customer, other searches would be difficult. To find all the people who have made a purchase in the last three months, or everyone who lives in a particular city, the retailer would have to sort through the file, card by card. For a relatively small file, this undertaking might not be too arduous, but some organizations have such voluminous records that paper searches would be impossibly time-consuming.

Record-keeping was one of the first commercial uses for computers. Those early databases, like many simple modern programs, were little more than computerized filing systems, holding the electronic equivalent of documents organized in folders and drawers. In modern databases, separate items of information, called fields, are organized into records, and records into

DATABASE

A database can be compared to a filing system containing many records. Each record is divided into categories called fields. Information can be rapidly located by searching through any index, or combination of indexes.

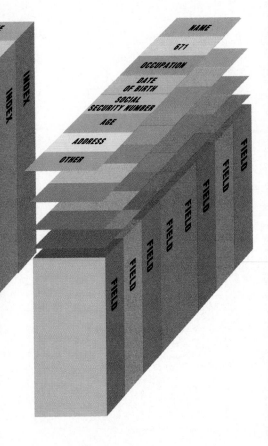

84

If the user wants to find all the doctors in this database, a search is conducted through the index for the single field: Profession. A single field search may produce many records.

To refine the search and look for doctors in a particular age group, a search is made through a second index, in this case the field: Age. A two-field search produces a smaller number of records.

To further narrow the query and find all the doctors in a particular age group who also have the same name, a search is made through a third index, for the field: Name. The program produces an even smaller number of records.

files. A personnel file, for example, contains a record for each employee that has several fields for such information as name, date of employment, or job title. A search for information can be made through any field, or combination of fields, in the database.

The initial search for any record is not normally made through the entire database. That would be far too time-consuming—like looking for one book in a huge library without consulting an index. A reader looking for all the novels by a particular author, for example, would in fact bypass the nonfiction and reference sections altogether. He would then consult the author index and the title index to locate the books—a process that resembles a database search. Usually, each field in the stack of records in a database can be assigned its own index. It is the index that is searched, not the database.

As computers gained more processing power and storage capacity, database management software improved as well. The most important gains were in flexibility, ease of access, and the ability to make connections between different pieces of information within a database. Some of the most advanced record-keeping programs are called relational database managers. These programs store facts in tables of rows and columns, each row like a single record in an ordinary database. Considered individually, a table is just a simple file of records. But if the user deliberately duplicates a column of data entries (social security numbers, for instance) in two or more tables, the program can link the tables together. The common key, as this special column is called, gives the user access to all the data in any table it occupies, allowing the construction of sophisticated reports involving many different kinds of information.

Databases can be used—provided the user asks the right question in the right way—to cross-reference any of the categories of information they contain at a keystroke. Most programs require the user to couch requests in a special query language, which embodies some of the powers of a programming language, using keywords to initiate complex actions. Although the ability to access and manipulate vast amounts of data was available before the advent of electronic computers, it was a demanding business, usually involving many people in days, weeks or months of work. Information retrieval through a database now puts access to massive amounts of information literally at the fingertips of the individual.

PAINTING BY NUMBERS

Computer graphics programs can help a homeowner draft plans for a new kitchen, provide hours of entertainment for the commander of an imaginary submarine, or conjure up possible answers for an astrophysicist probing the mysteries of galactic origins. The often dazzling images the software produces tend to overshadow the utilitarian benefits that many programs provide. While some are aimed at nothing more than making pictures, others use the pictures to facilitate all kinds of jobs. But whatever its use, graphics software is typically so complex that it requires hundreds of thousands of lines of code, developed over many years.

The simplest graphics-based software are the drawing and painting programs used to produce images on the screen. For these programs, the images are the end product, whether they are to be printed on paper, transferred to film, or incorporated into other programs. At their most fundamental level, drawing and painting

GRAPHIC POSSIBILITIES

Graphic programs allow designers and artists to draw images on the screen. The images can be changed, moved and manipulated with ease, providing far greater flexibility and speed than traditional methods.

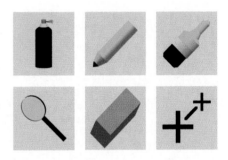

Icons are a symbolic way of representing commands on the screen. For example, to give the command to enlarge an image, the user would select the magnifying glass icon with an input tool such as a mouse.

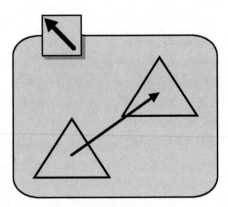

Typical functions found in a graphics program include **move**, **draw circle**, **rotate** and **fill**. To shift an image from one part of the screen to another *(above)*, the user selects the move icon from an on-screen palette.

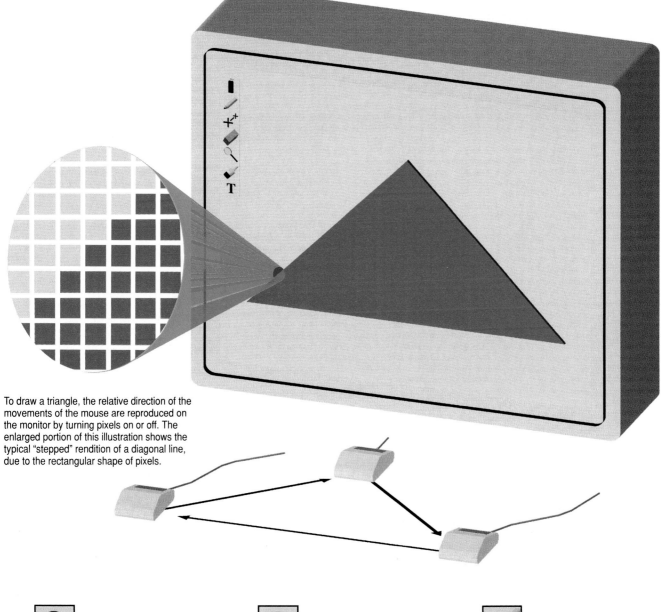

To draw a triangle, the relative direction of the movements of the mouse are reproduced on the monitor by turning pixels on or off. The enlarged portion of this illustration shows the typical "stepped" rendition of a diagonal line, due to the rectangular shape of pixels.

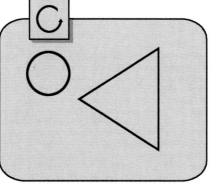

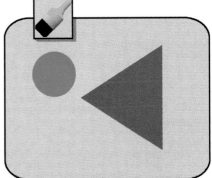

Drawing a freehand circle to add to the triangle is difficult, but with a graphics program, the user simply selects the draw circle command, and defines the screen coordinates of the center and radius with the mouse.

To move the image of the triangle around its axis, the user selects the rotate command.

Once the outline of an image is drawn, it can be colored or shaded by using the fill command. Colors and textures are selected from an on-screen palette.

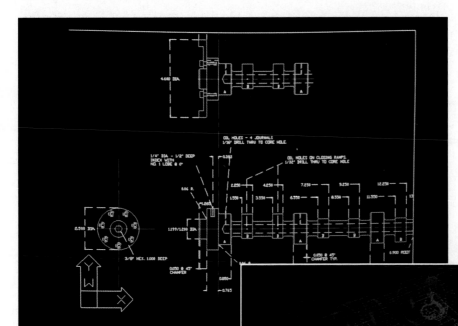

The first step in creating a drawing with a computer-aided design (CAD) program is to make a traditional image in the style of a blueprint. The example at left shows three views of the object.

Next, the program generates a wire frame rendering of the design as it would appear in three dimensions (below).

Finally, the program performs solid modeling on the wire frame, which renders the object's appearance in different lighting conditions.

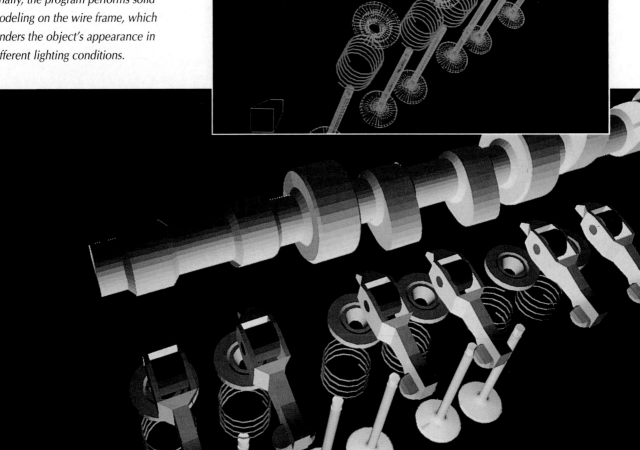

programs are tool kits for changing the colors of tiny rectangles on the screen called pixels (for picture elements). The thousands of pixels on a black-and-white screen, for example, are turned on or off in patterns that add up to a picture. A color image is more complicated, since the program must control the color of each pixel, drawing from a palette that may include hundreds or thousands of hues.

For the user, the software is similar in many ways to applying paint to paper or canvas. From a menu on the screen, the artist selects a tool such as a brush, determines its shape and width, and assigns it a color. Then, controlling the screen tool by moving an input device such as a mouse, a trackball or a digitizing pad and stylus, the artist creates dots, lines or swaths of color across the screen. The brush is only one of the available instruments. Most programs also provide electronic erasers for selective or total removal of previous work, airbrushes for delicate shading of colors and text tools for inserting type into the image. The program interprets the input according to the tool in use, then processes the new data with the information it already has about the image on the screen. It then recreates the image in a separate video memory in RAM, pixel by pixel. Finally, the contents of this memory are converted to a screen image.

Painting and drawing programs are called interactive when they respond directly and almost instantaneously to the user's commands. But many graphics-oriented programs use a different approach. Instead of providing the artist with familiar

FROM PIXEL TO PROTOTYPE

The output technique called sintering brings together elements of three different disciplines: chemistry, laser control and computer graphics. The sintering machine receives its instructions from a CAD file, which directs a flashing laser beam to scan a layer of plastic powder in a cylinder. The laser heat-fuses the powder into a solid form wherever it touches down. Each layer of solid plastic is an exact cross section of the object to be produced. The cylinder then drops down, lowering the wafer of fused plastic. Next, a roller deposits a new coating of plastic powder on top of the solid cross section and the process is repeated until the output takes its completed shape. By building up the solid output in wafer-thin strata—slices of reality—the prototype takes shape as a detailed solid model, including interior features, from the bottom up.

A scanner skims a powdered medium and turns a pinpoint laser on and off. Wherever the beam hits the medium, it fuses a cross section of a CAD design into a thin solid layer, building up a finished prototype layer by layer.

From Revolution to Routine

It has been called a revolutionary and democratizing technology. And for once the hyperbole is surpassed by reality. Desktop publishing—the union of word processing, computer graphics and high-resolution printing in one small and affordable package—has changed the way everything from business cards to books is published. Desktop publishing is revolutionary because it bypasses steps that for centuries have been handled almost exclusively by trained professionals: design, typesetting, paste-up and often printing. And it is democratizing because it puts these skills into the hands of anyone who has learned to use a computer.

The marriage of text and graphics in one software program has been around since the early 1970s. But it was the arrival of Apple Computer's LaserWriter in 1985 that sparked the desktop publishing phenomenon. This new printer, working in concert with a text-graphics program on a microcomputer, allowed one individual to write, design and typeset professional-quality pages on a single system. And unlike earlier laser printers, the LaserWriter could adjust type fonts to virtually any size.

To begin a desktop publishing document, the user chooses the specific dimensions of the page to be designed, and the screen then becomes an electronic paste-up board. With a few keystrokes, a text file is brought directly onto the screen. While the computer keeps track of the proper word order, the user moves text freely on the electronic page, one word at a time or in large blocks. The text can be laid out in any number of columns and changed to a particular typeface at a specific size. The options, from large headlines to small photo credits, are limitless. At this stage, art may be added, whether it takes the form of electronically scanned photographs or graphics drawn on screen. Like text, pictures also may be moved, enlarged, reduced, or cropped, and the user can draw lines of varying thickness, create assorted shapes and add shading. The essence of this process goes by the acronym WYSIWYG, for "what you see is what you get." Whatever appears on the screen is very similar to what the printed page will look like.

At any time during the process the laser printer can provide a good quality printout that serves as either a draft or a final page—a huge time-saving over traditional methods. Before desktop publishing, a writer would compose copy, a typesetter would produce printed text, and a designer would cut up the columns of type, strip in graphics and lay out the pages on art boards. Then those boards would be sent to professional printers. With a desktop publishing program, the final laser-printed pages are sent directly to a printing house or simply photocopied by the user.

These programs have rapidly made their mark. They are used by individuals, by corporate communications departments, and by some major newspapers. Indeed, many new word processing programs now include layout features.

In just a few short years, the revolution has become routine, but for all its democratizing aspects, desktop publishing is not creativity in a package. It has not eliminated the need for skilled designers any more than word processing has put good writers out of work. As the programs become even more widely used, the "desktop" may be dropped and the entire process known—once again—simply as publishing.

tools, they respond to lists of instructions, creating the image only after the user has specified its many elements. For example, the artist may specify the radius, position, color and surface texture of a sphere. The program then does the mathematical computations required to transform the commands into patterns of pixels, and draws the sphere on the screen. Programs used to animate special effects for movies often incorporate functions for painting natural shapes, such as a clump of grass or the branches of a tree, that would take far too long to render by hand. Instead, the artist tells the program where to begin. The program does the rest, using techniques that introduce a degree of randomness into the shapes and generating amazingly realistic images.

THE POWER OF CAD AND CAM

The attributes of drawing programs are combined with mathematical and data-handling functions in software used to draw plans for everything from houses to machine tools. Computer-aided design (CAD) programs can display blueprints and three-dimensional images on the screen, rotating them on command to provide different perspectives to the viewer. CAD software also keeps track of the precise characteristics of every component of a design, so that each time the user changes an element on the screen, the program can recalculate its dimensions. Most CAD programs also include a database of stock parts, which the designer can insert into a drawing with a single command. An architect, for example, can indicate positions for all the appliances and fixtures in a kitchen, leaving it to the CAD software to get the dimensions right. On a larger scale, the architect can use CAD to produce images of an entire building, and view it from any angle in any lighting conditions. The counterpart of CAD is CAM: computer-aided manufacture. CAM programs send instructions from CAD directly to automated production lines. CAD and CAM have transformed design and production techniques as irrevocably as the Industrial Revolution changed entire societies and economies.

Graphics also merge with mathematics in software used to simulate natural phenomena, particularly those that are unsuitable for experimental investigation because of their size, their pace or their remoteness. Researchers program simulations by entering into the computer the equations that they believe govern the process they are studying, then solving the equations and comparing the results to their empirical observations. Thus, a scientist simulating the evolution of a star would compare the computer's final version of the star with a real one. The closer the match, the more likely it is that the equations used in the simulation are correct.

In many simulations, however, the results are so complex that they would be almost impossible to understand if they were simply listed in numerical tables. A typical problem in astrophysics, for example, might involve as many as a million imaginary particles, each with a velocity and position changing over time. Representing the interactions of all these particles might take 10 million intertwined equations. Only by linking the equations to graphics and presenting the results as a sort of hypothetical movie, can scientists grasp the outcome of their simulations. Making the films, however, is almost as hard as doing the computations in the first place. Researchers who computed the collapse of a star cluster into a black hole found that even a brief sequence of images required 10 hours of labor by a Cray X-MP, a powerful supercomputer.

The trend in software is to put the kind of power and clarity embodied in programs such as these at the disposal of every computer user. Simulation software and CAD programs have migrated to microcomputers, their powers scaled back but nevertheless impressive. Graphics have also begun to change the face of word processing: desktop publishing (DTP) puts images of the finished document onto the screen, with pictures and headlines in place, ready to be printed out with extraordinary crispness by a laser printer. The full impact of desktop publishing remains to be seen, but many have speculated that there will be a further explosion of a wide variety of new publications aimed at readerships both large and small. The ability to turn out professional-quality newsletters and magazines from a home office makes DTP a powerful medium previously only at the disposal of large organizations.

Continuing advances in computer hardware allow software designers to add such features, increasing the power and flexibility of their programs. But making things easier for the user often means making things tougher for the programmer. Bringing a complex program to market can take years of work by hundreds of programmers. Furthermore, for all its power, the new software is often tricky to use, every program responding to its own special command set and working only on the jobs for which it was designed. Because customizing software for new jobs takes the same kind of effort that goes into the original programming, most users adapt their work to the capabilities of their software, rather than vice versa. Though these problems are more of a nuisance than a serious setback, this is a state of affairs that may be short-lived, as programmers search for methods to make software more adaptable.

OBJECT-ORIENTED PROGRAMMING

The solutions are beginning to take shape in new software, some of which allows even nontechnical users to shape their own programs without having to write any code or understand a computer language. The underlying principle of these new systems is known as object-oriented programming, a technique that treats all the elements of a program as separate modules, called objects. Each object contains its own data as well as procedures for handling that data. A circle object in a paint program, for example, would contain a value for its radius plus instructions for drawing a circle. In effect, each object is a small, specialized program that does its job every time it is called on, without revealing its inner workings to the outside world.

Because an object can contain any segment of a program—even something as complicated as a text editor—an object-oriented program can put enormous power at the disposal of even the least computer-wise person. When objects are portrayed graphically, they lend substance to abstract data and procedures, inviting the user to test new arrangements for the elements of the system simply by moving them or linking them on the screen. This kind of interactive programming can lead to new ways of doing old jobs, and even to new jobs that were never before imagined. And by removing the need to understand computers, the new software helps bring the machines to a new level of utility. Instead of adapting themselves and their work to the finicky standards of computers, more and more people will use software to shape computers to their needs.

STORAGE

The work done by a computer would be useless if it were to disappear at the end of the work session. Yet that is exactly what would happen in most computers if the work was left in RAM, the machine's temporary memory. RAM is designed to accommodate the task at hand, but is operational only so long as the power is switched on. The instant the power goes off, whether by accident or design, RAM is once more an empty slate. To use and re-use programs and files from session to session, the user must "save" a newly created or freshly updated document to storage, an electronic filing system that will keep its contents in order, even with the power off.

Modern computers make use of two storage technologies—magnetic and optical. Data storage methods relying on magnetism have predominated through most of electronic computing history with optical technology only coming on the scene in the 1970s.

All magnetic storage operates on the principle that atoms of certain elements—chiefly iron, nickel, chromium and cobalt—act as natural magnets. When a disk, drum or tape is coated with a powdered alloy of one of these elements, usually iron dioxide, the magnetized atoms behave like microscopic bar magnets, each generating its own field. Ordinarily, the millions of individual fields have the net effect of canceling each other out, but if a stronger magnetic field—which can be produced by an electrical current flowing through an electromagnet—is applied to the atoms, they will obligingly line up in the direction, or polarity, of the external magnetic lines of force. When current is reversed, the magnetic field follows suit. Magnetic polarity can line up magnetized atoms in one of only two directions—a phenomenon that conveniently corresponds with the binary code. Data can thus be recorded simply by alternating the magnetic field of the coating of storage disk or tape.

Tape was an early magnetic medium which continues to be used widely for backup and for archival storage of data. Borrowed from the music recording industry, tape was a great leap forward. One drawback, however, is that taped infor-

---

Just as a library offers readers access to stored books, a computer enables users to keep their work in a repository that is well organized and indexed for rapid access.

mation is stored—and recovered—in serial fashion, which means that finding a given piece of data can be a frustratingly slow process.

Magnetic drums, spinning metal cylinders introduced in the late 1950s, organized data in parallel tracks that significantly reduced the time needed to find a stored item. Drums had limited capacity, however, and by the end of the 1960s they had been supplanted by hard disks—rigid metallic platters two feet in diameter. Disks offered faster access to data and could store up to 200 megabytes, the equivalent of 60,000 single-spaced, typewritten pages.

In 1971, IBM introduced the considerably smaller, flexible magnetic disk, the now commonplace floppy. At just eight inches across, the floppy was one-third the diameter of a hard disk, and it could only accommodate a minute percentage (250 kilobytes) of the information that could be stored on a hard disk. These first flexible disks were the precursors of those used in today's home computers.

Since their debuts, both hard and floppy disks have shrunk steadily in size and just as steadily grown in capacity. The smallest floppy disks, at 3.5 inches, can hold as much as 1.44 megabytes of data, while a hard disk of the same size can store at least 40 times that amount of information. A newer 3.5-inch hard disk system might hold as much as 500 megabytes; a slightly larger system using 5.25-inch platters can store hundreds or thousands of megabytes.

KEEPING TRACKS

As magnetic storage has evolved, the capacity of a magnetic disk has become a function of what is termed its density, rather than its diameter. A disk holds data in concentric circles called tracks; the more tracks per inch, the denser the disk. Modern floppy disks range from 48 to 135 tracks per square inch, while hard disks may have anywhere from 300 to 2,000 tracks per square inch. Tracks are further subdivided into sectors; thus, a schematized view would depict the disk as an evenly sliced pie. High-density disks divide their tracks into more sectors. For example, the standard, double-density 5.25-inch floppy disk that is one of the mainstays in today's personal computers can hold 360 kilobytes in between 48 and 96 tracks per inch and 9 sectors. A high-density version stores 1.2 megabytes in 96 tracks per inch and either 9 or 15 sectors.

The outermost track of each disk is set aside for a directory, or index, of the files stored on the disk by track and sector, leaving the remaining tracks for data storage. Despite this seemingly tidy arrangement of tracks and sectors, a disk-based system takes a somewhat haphazard approach to the storage of data. A disk drive will tuck a block of data into any available track on the disk—which can leave related data blocks strewn across the surface of the disk. However, the small size of a magnetic disk means that no matter how widely dispersed the stored bits of data are, they can never be more than a few inches apart. Moreover, in filing away data, the disk drive leaves itself an electronic trail, noting the address of each block in the appropriate directory and thus ensuring that it can easily piece together the various parts of a file. The directory ensures that the computer can retrieve any requested block of data almost instantaneously: 160 milliseconds on a floppy disk, a mere nine milliseconds on a hard disk.

The storage and retrieval of information on magnetic disks are carried out by disk drives employing electromagnetic read/write heads. To store, or write, data on a disk, electrical pulses passed through the heads magnetize the surface of the disk in the direction of the applied current.

Each pair of pulses is translated into two bands of magnetism that together make up a single bit cell on the tape or disk. In order for the storage device to differentiate between data bits, the first band in each bit cell always reverses the polarity of the previous band. The second band will have the same polarity if the stored bit is a zero, or it will reverse the polarity at midcell if the bit is a one. In reading the data, the read/write head senses these midcell changes in the magnetic field. Thus, a midcell reversal of polarity will induce an electrical pulse in the electromagnet that will be read by the computer as a binary one. The absence of a reversal—indicating that both bands of a bit cell are magnetized in the same direction—will be read as a zero, since no current will be induced in the electromagnet.

READ/WRITE HEADS

In a floppy disk drive, two read/write heads supported by a forked actuator arm access the top and underside of the disk. As a drive motor spins the disk at 300 revolutions per minute, a stepper motor moves the actuator arm in a straight line, to position the heads precisely at a selected sector and track.

The read/write heads themselves vary somewhat in design, depending on the type of disk drive. Each consists of three separate heads. A single read/write head for recording and retrieving data is sandwiched between two erase heads, whose sole purpose is to remove any stray magnetic signals from the area on either side of a data track. The resulting demagnetized zones not only isolate the data track, but also help to compensate for any variations in alignment between different disk drives, ensuring that data recorded by one drive will be readable by another.

The read/write heads of all floppy disk drives must actually touch the surface of a disk in order to record or retrieve data. To do so, the heads use a small access window cut into the protective jacket enclosing the disk. This window, obvious on a 5.25-inch floppy, is hidden beneath a spring-loaded door on a 3.5-inch disk and is only exposed when the disk is inserted into a disk drive. A smaller, round hole, called the index hole, punched in the jacket of a 5.25-inch floppy and in the disk itself, provides a reference point for the reading and writing of data; magnetic signals recorded in a special location on a 3.5-inch disk serve the same purpose in lieu of an index hole. Both kinds of floppies also incorporate what is known as a write-protect feature to prevent data from being written over or accidentally erased. On a 5.25-inch disk this feature takes the form of a notch cut into one side of the disk's protective jacket made of the plastic material PVC; covering the notch with a small piece of tape allows the disk to be read but not written to. On a 3.5-inch floppy, a tab in one corner of the disk can be slid open to prevent the disk from being written to.

To protect sensitive data from irrevocable loss, a special lining inside the jacket sweeps the surface of the disk as it spins, collecting dust and bits of magnetic material as they are shed by the disk. To a disk drive, a particle of dust the size of a bacterium looms as large as a boulder and can all too easily disrupt the reading and writing of data. A human hair, measuring just 40 microns thick, has the same potential for disaster as a log across a superhighway and can wreak similarly devastating havoc.

THE READ/WRITE HEAD

The read/write head reads information from the rotating disk by recognizing changes in the direction of magnetism on its surface. The head writes information to the disk by magnetizing its surface in the direction of the current applied.

When there is no change in the direction of the magnetism between successive cells, the head recognizes a zero.

The read/write head recognizes a one by sensing a change in the magnetic direction on the cell that is passing under it.

Inevitably, some of the microscopic litter escapes the lining and gradually accumulates in the recording gap that forms part of a read/write head. In time enough debris can build up to clog the gap, leading to read/write errors and eventually rendering the head useless. A special head-cleaning disk may remedy the problem and reduce the likelihood of disk or head failure.

FLOATING ON AIR

A hard-disk system incorporates a drive motor capable of spinning the system's disks at a dizzying 3,600 revolutions per minute and a stepper motor that controls an actuator arm with a read/write head mounted at the tip. The shaft of the drive motor is attached directly to the platters, rather than to a turntable, and the actuator arm moves across the disk in an arc. The read/write heads of a hard-disk system, like those in a floppy drive, are arranged in pairs, with one head for the top surface of each platter and the other for each underside. The rapid rotation of the disk creates a cushion of air that measures a mere 20 millionths of an inch in depth. Magnetic principles govern the actual transfer of data to and from the disk as the paired heads, or sliders, float near the surface of the disk on the cushion of air. The fact that there is no physical contact between the disk and the read/write heads reduces the potential for wear and tear on both. Unintentional contact, however, is another matter. Surface debris, for example, can wreak havoc with a hard-disk system if it manages to invade the system's sealed housing and elude the drive's built-in air-filtration system. Even a particle of cigarette smoke can be a large enough obstacle in the cushion of air a slider rides on to upset its equilibrium and send it careening toward the surface of the disk. The resulting "head crash"—the microscopic equivalent of a 60-mile-per-hour, head-on collision—can scrape off the disk's magnetic coating, destroying data and damaging the head itself.

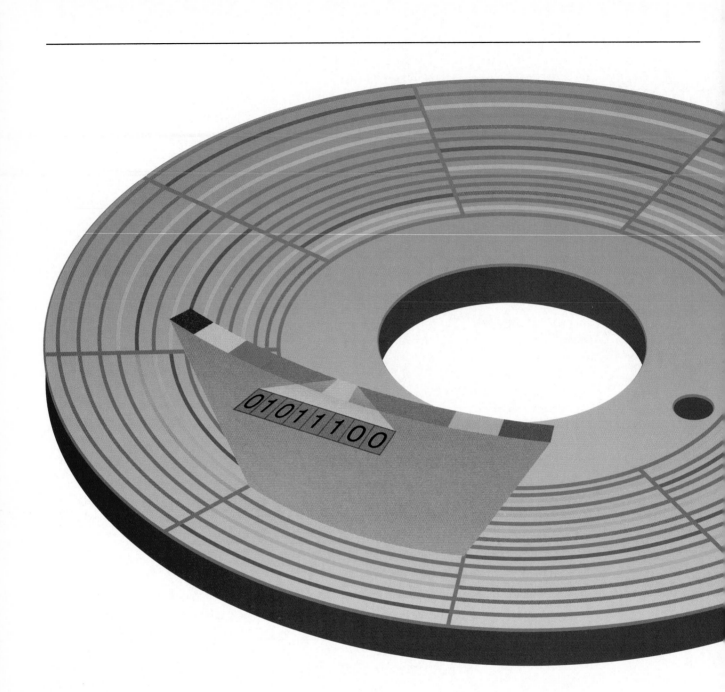

MAKING LIGHT WORK

One way to avoid the physical and electronic mayhem brought on by a head crash is to use a nonmagnetic storage device that is virtually impervious to such mishaps—the optical disk drive.

As its name suggests, an optical-disk system uses light, rather than magnetism, to record and retrieve stored data. At the core of the system is a read/write head made up of a laser and an array of lenses that train its beam onto a spinning disk. One form of optical disk is a 4.75-inch plastic-and-aluminum sandwich called CD-ROM, for Compact Disk-Read Only Memory. It resembles an audio compact disk in appearance and function, and with a capacity of 656 megabytes, a CD-ROM disk can hold more than 1,300 times as much information as a similarly sized double-density floppy. This advance in capacity over magnetic disks, coupled

DISK ORGANIZATION

Magnetic disks are organized in a series of concentric circles called tracks. Radial lines further divide the disk into sectors. Each intersection of the tracks and sectors is called a block, and is given a unique number to serve as its address. The address allows information stored in any block to be readily located.

FRAGMENTATION

The computer stores information anywhere it finds an unused block on a disk. As a result, different parts of the same document or file may end up spread throughout the disk *(below, left).*

This fragmentation builds up over time as the disk is filled. The more a disk is fragmented, the longer it takes for the computer to load all the blocks belonging to one file into memory. Defragmentation places related blocks adjacent to each other *(below, right).* Some computer systems will do this automatically, while others need a separate utility program.

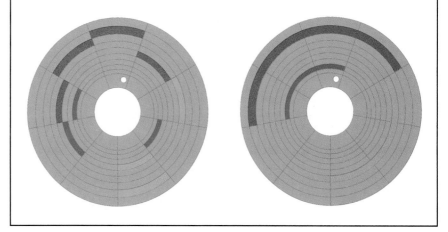

with enhanced durability, makes CD-ROM a practical storage medium. What truly sets it apart from magnetic disks, however, is that its increased capacity makes it possible to use CD-ROM to store sound and images as well as text, in a compact, reliable and portable package. CD-ROMs, however, can serve up only the information recorded on them during manufacturing; they cannot be written to. Another form of optical storage, Write Once, Read Many (WORM), can be written to once and read from repeatedly. But it is possible to encode and erase information as often as desired using yet another format—hybrids called magneto-optic disks that rely on a laser and the inherent magnetism of one of several kinds of alloys.

All three kinds of optical disks are laminates of plastic and a metallic or organic (carbon-based) compound; the metallic disks are used in read-only applications, the organic compounds for read-and-write disks. A cross section of a CD-ROM, for example, would expose a layer of plastic, topped with a layer of reflective aluminum and then a final protective layer of plastic. Microscopic examination of the same disk would reveal one of two kinds of tracks, packed 16,000 to the inch: either concentric circles, like those of a magnetic disk, or a single, tightly coiled spiral, which, if it could be unwound, would stretch some three miles in length.

During the recording process, data is encoded along the tracks as long, narrow depressions on one side of the smooth optical disk. On the underside of the disk, where the information will be read by the laser beam, the depressions protrude downward as flat-topped bumps. Nevertheless, in optical storage parlance, these protrusions are called pits. As many as two billion pits can be crammed onto a single disk. Between each pit is a flat area known as a land. Connecting the pits and lands are sloping transition areas, not unlike the grade of a hill.

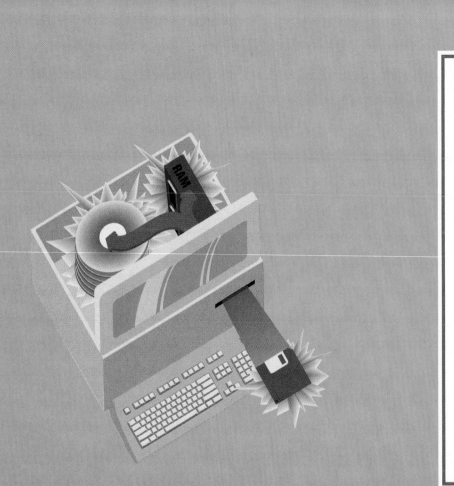

Binary Sabotage

They have names that range from banal to sinister: No-Name; Pakistani Brain; Stoned; Plastique; Data Crime; Devil's Dance; and Dark Avenger. Some are relatively harmless to computers. Others wreak havoc throughout huge electronic networks, causing millions of dollars worth of damage. But whatever the particular name or function, computer viruses have become a fact of life, and all machines—from personal computers to huge mainframes—may be regarded as vulnerable.

Often consisting of only a few lines of code, a virus is a program designed to infect larger programs, and then to create clones of itself. Each replica in turn seeks out new hosts. Some viruses become Trojan horses; once inside a system they eliminate as much data as possible. Other varieties alter data, slowing down or disrupting the flow of infor-

The most common carrier of computer viruses is the floppy disk, although some systems may become infected through modems or by other computers in networks.

Once a virus is in the system, it will affect RAM. As long as the computer is turned on, RAM serves as a base from which the virus will spread. It will seek to infect permanent storage devices such as other floppy disks, hard disks or tape drives.

mation. Even viruses meant only to bring humorous messages to monitors can get out of control and damage a whole system.

Viruses are able to carry out their nefarious deeds because computers obediently follow instructions. A computer cannot know whether a virus is a hacker's jest, a malicious piece of sabotage or a legitimate command. To the machine, program code is program code. Once inside the system, a virus' instructions will be followed by the computer as if they were part of the original program.

The most common virus carrier is the floppy disk. Pirated software, public domain programs or borrowed disks all may be contaminated. If the virus then moves from the floppy to a PC's hard disk, or any other permanent storage device, it has found a base from which to infect new programs as they are installed.

The ability to spread rapidly, potentially infecting thousands of machines, is what makes a virus so dangerous. When computers are connected by modems or in electron-ic networks, the stage is set for a widespread viral outbreak.

Like all digital information, a virus can travel instantly over telephone lines to enter receptive machines. It can piggyback on legitimate files or be programmed to command the computer to send it. Although most systems require passwords, some viruses cunningly find ways to gain access. The notorious Internet Virus, which immobilized more than 6,000 NASA, Air Force and university network computers across the USA in 1988, knocked on each computer's door with 432 different passwords.

Like their biological namesakes, computer viruses will never be eliminated. But computer scientists have devised lines of defence against them. Antiviral programs seek out suspicious additions to a system and some of these programs will remove viruses automatically. For the personal computer user, though, the best plan is to swear off what has become an accepted habit—using illegally pirated software.

The virus may strike out from one computer to others linked in a network. Computers thousands of miles away can become infected if they are connected to a diseased machine through a modem.

When the computer is turned off, and RAM disappears, the virus resides in permanent storage and waits for an opportunity to spread.

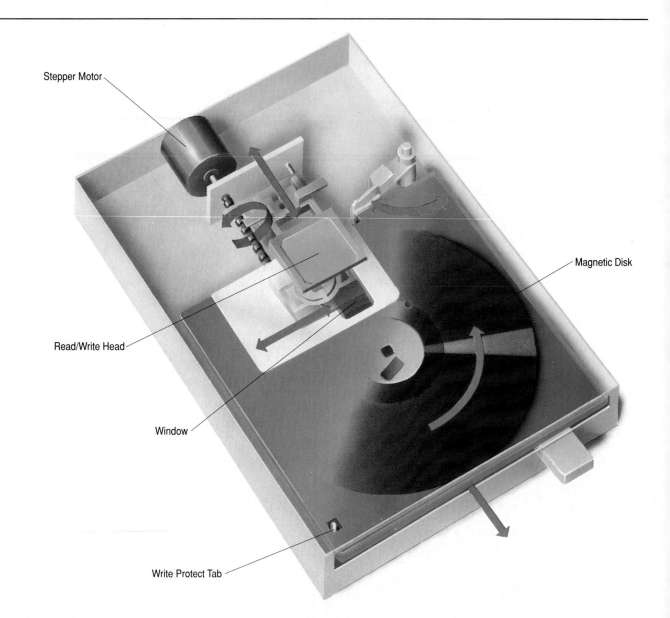

Stepper Motor

Magnetic Disk

Read/Write Head

Window

Write Protect Tab

To read a CD-ROM, the laser in the optical drive funnels its light through a series of lenses and a beam splitter until it is focused to a point just one micron in diameter. This pinprick of light is then directed onto the underside of the spinning disk, where it locks onto a data track. Whenever the beam strikes a flat land or the flat surface of a pit, the light is reflected, at different intensities, back along its original path and then diverted to a photodetector. In either case, the light is translated and interpreted as a binary zero. The transition areas, on the other hand, scatter most of the laser's beam so that very little of the light is bounced back to the photodetector. The laser reads these transition areas as binary ones. As the laser continues to arc along the data track, the constantly shifting intensity of the reflected beam is translated by the photodetector into a signal that can then be interpreted by the optical drive's circuitry as a series of binary ones and zeros. The length of the pits and lands determines how many zeros are registered.

As with other storage technologies, there has been a time lag of several years between the initial development of optical storage for computers and its subse-

FLOPPY DISK DRIVE

The 3.5-inch disk drive stores data and retrieves it from removable magnetic disks. Floppy disks lack the capacity of hard disks, but can be conveniently used in any number of computers.

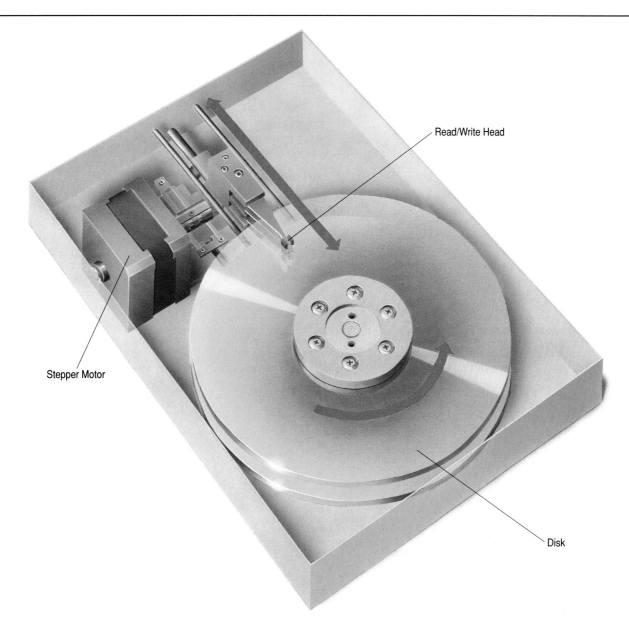

Read/Write Head

Stepper Motor

Disk

HARD DISK DRIVE

The hard disk drive is a sealed unit containing rigid nonremovable disks for data storage and retrieval. The storage capacity and speed of access of hard disks far exceed the capabilities of floppy drives.

quent entry into the PC market. The NeXT computer, introduced in January 1989—and initially offered for sale to colleges—was the first machine to be marketed with a built-in optical disk drive. Its removable disk holds 256 megabytes of data and, unlike CD-ROM, can be written to. At the start of the 1990s two other computer companies, HeadStart and Tandy, introduced machines with built-in CD-ROM drives aimed at the home user.

By 1990 there were an estimated 900 commercially available prerecorded disks. The catalogue for home use includes reference works such as encyclopedias, dictionaries, atlases and literary works—one featured the full text of Sir Arthur Conan Doyle's Sherlock Holmes stories, packaged with their original illustrations from The Strand Magazine. For business, professional and academic use, there are packages that range from financial data on companies to a CD-ROM for health care professionals that lists 500,000 toxic substances and their antidotes.

One of the most promising developments in optical technology is called digital paper, which also uses a laser to read and write data. Digital paper takes its name from the fact that it is manufactured in large sheets and rolls that can then be fashioned into reels of tape, disks or even wallet-sized optical-memory cards. Yet despite its name, it is actually a thin-film composite built up from layers of polyester, reflective metal and heat-absorbent dyes. Cut and shaped into a 12-inch reel of 35-mm optical tape, for example, it has a tremendous capacity of one terabyte, or a thousand gigabytes, dwarfing by far the capacity of any other storage device. The entire Bible—laser-encoded as tiny holes or dimples in the coated tape—fits into a space only slightly larger than the head of a pin, while a single reel of optical paper can hold as many as two million 500-page books or one billion double-spaced typed pages. While this new technology is undeniably promising, it is not yet established as a medium of storage, and it may never be. Its fate is for the near future to decide.

PITS AND LANDS

This close-up view of an optical disk shows the protrusions—called pits—that are made on the underside of an optical disk when it is recorded. The spaces between pits are called lands. A laser beam follows the recorded data tracks on a disk, but its reflected light (red arrows) behaves differently depending on whether it strikes the flat areas of a protrusion or a land (above, left), or whether it bounces off the sloping side of the transition areas between land and pits (above, right). The optical drive reads the light signals from lands and pits as binary zeros. Signals from transition areas are read as binary ones.

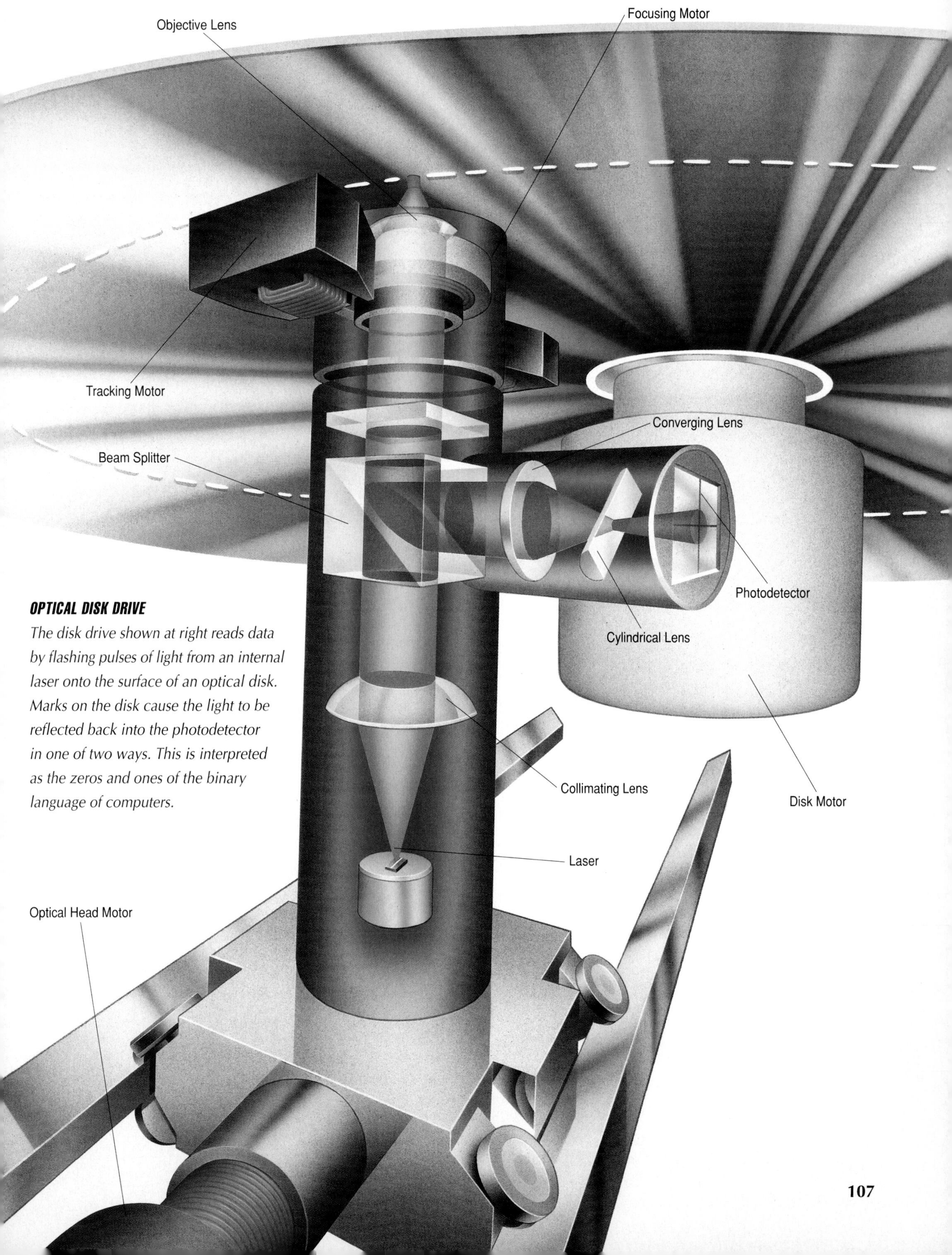

Objective Lens

Focusing Motor

Tracking Motor

Beam Splitter

Converging Lens

Photodetector

Cylindrical Lens

OPTICAL DISK DRIVE

*The disk drive shown at right reads data
by flashing pulses of light from an internal
laser onto the surface of an optical disk.
Marks on the disk cause the light to be
reflected back into the photodetector
in one of two ways. This is interpreted
as the zeros and ones of the binary
language of computers.*

Collimating Lens

Disk Motor

Laser

Optical Head Motor

Multimedia

A young music student slips a thin silver platter into a disk drive and the image of Wolfgang Amadeus Mozart appears on her screen. She clicks icons with a mouse and calls up pictures, video images and text about the composer. Next she asks for music and hears it through speakers connected to the computer. Now she listens to excerpts from sonatas while following corresponding musical notations on the screen. Her next request is for spoken commentary by an expert on Mozart. All of this information is at the student's fingertips as she pursues new lines of questions and areas of interest. She controls the pace and determines the path she will take; what she discovers along the way is very much in her own hands.

This scenario is an example of a state-of-the-art multimedia system—the combination of graphics, text, sound and video display running interactively on a desktop computer. Multimedia is not a machine, nor is it a program. Rather, it is innovative software, new hardware and some reliable older technology working in unison. The essential components of a multimedia system are a computer with a built-in or external optical disk drive, a high resolution screen, a powerful sound card, speakers and a program to coordinate it all.

The merging of sound and images into a single medium is not new; film and video have long done that. But in a multimedia set-up, the various media are brought together on a desktop, thanks largely to the optical disk and its enormous storage capacity. Originally developed in the late 1970s, the optical or compact disk is best known as an alternative to records and tapes. But images and words, as well as music, can be imprinted on an optical disk through laser technology. A typical 4.7-inch optical disk holds as much information as 1,300 standard floppy disks—more than 250,000 pages of text, eight hours of speech or music and 2,000 high-resolution images. Twelve-inch laser disks that hold much more information have a greater capacity. And because it is all packed into one neat unit, a user can move easily from one medium to another.

Software producers have taken advantage of this versatility to produce ever more interactive multimedia programs. Encyclopedias are an example of the new multimedia software packages. One electronic multi-disk encyclopedia includes text articles, spoken segments of famous speeches, 15,000 photographs, charts and diagrams and an hour of recorded music. Even the irreverent Whole Earth Catalogue—complete with recorded birdsong—has made it onto optical disk.

Perhaps the most worthwhile aspect of multimedia is its potential as an educational tool. Most people, especially children, absorb new information in a cooperative, nonlinear fashion; learning does not necessarily begin at page one. Multimedia educational programs are increasingly available for primary and secondary schools. Some companies have made special training disks for their sales personnel. On their screens, new employees encounter different situations and scenarios as they work with the program; a certain decision brings a whole new set of circumstances in the next scenario. Multimedia systems also are being used in the aerospace and medical professions as training tools for pilots and surgeons.

Affordable, fully interactive multimedia systems are still in their infancy, however. Video images consume an enormous amount of storage space and are not yet a viable desktop option. Still, as its popularity grows, multimedia will become cheaper, more accessible and—many believe—commonplace.

The impressive storage capacity of optical disks has led to the development of interactive systems that combine text, sound, graphic and video displays.

OUTPUT

The visual effect is stunning. A giant kaleidoscopic motion picture show is playing in the stands of a stadium in broad daylight. Yet there is no film, no projector and no screen. The display is not even plugged into the electrical supply. This is a strictly people-powered event. The crowd is doing it all, by flashing colored rectangles in a disciplined, programmed sequence. Each card means nothing in itself, but when all the cards are viewed together as a whole, the result is a moving, ever-changing mosaic of surprising sophistication. The spectacle also happens to be an apt analogy for the way a computer generates visual output.

In many respects, output is the reverse process of input. When the computer crunches numbers in the recesses of its circuitry, it produces a result that is also numerical, and therefore meaningless to the user. Creating comprehensible output involves translating binary code back into a form that is familiar to people, such as graphs on a screen, words printed on paper or music pouring from loudspeakers. The output devices responsible for such variety take many forms, from the exotic to the workaday, but the most common are the familiar printer and the ubiquitous video display terminal, or monitor.

The image in the stadium is created in a way that mimics the monitor screen. But before the monitor can deliver the electronic goods, there must be a transformation from digital data byte to analog video signal. This conversion is set in motion when the CPU hands off a byte of data—together with control codes specifying how that data should look on the screen—to the computer's video memory, which holds about a screen's worth of data at a time. From there the data, still in the form of binary ones and zeros, is channeled to a set of chips making up the computer's display controller, which converts the computer's binary output into equivalent video signals. The signals are then flashed to the monitor itself.

What happens next depends on what kind of monitor receives the signals. Most of today's monitors are based on the tried-and-true technology of the cathode-ray tube, or CRT—the same technology that makes television possible. First invent-

These spectators in a Moscow stadium are part of the spectacle. By manipulating colored rectangles, they have become human pixels in an imitation of a computer display screen.

ed in the 1930s, the CRT consists of a conical sealed glass tube, with an electron-emitting gun set in the narrow end and a phosphorescent screen at the wide end. The screen itself is composed of horizontal rows and vertical columns of tiny rectangular picture elements, or pixels. The pixels are made up of cells coated with phosphors—chemicals that glow when exposed to electrons. The sharpness of the image is determined by the number of pixels in the screen. A typical 14-inch low-resolution screen for a personal computer has 128,000 pixels. These turn on and off—dozens of times each second—in response to a beam of electrons generated by the electron gun. Each phosphor-coated pixel has a corresponding address in the computer's video memory, so the image on the screen mirrors the contents of the memory unit.

POINTILLISM BY PIXEL

The images projected by a CRT get their start as electrical signals from the display controller that are relayed to an electromagnetic yoke surrounding the narrow neck of the CRT. Fluctuations in those signals reflect variations in the computer's binary output and trigger corresponding changes in the magnetic field generated by the yoke, deflecting and distorting the flow of electrons from the gun to the screen. As the electron beam of a monochrome CRT scans the screen row by row, moving

LIQUID CRYSTAL DISPLAY

The backlit LCD consists of components that are placed on both sides of the "sandwich" making up the screen. Pixels are created by applying current to electrodes at screen coordinates.

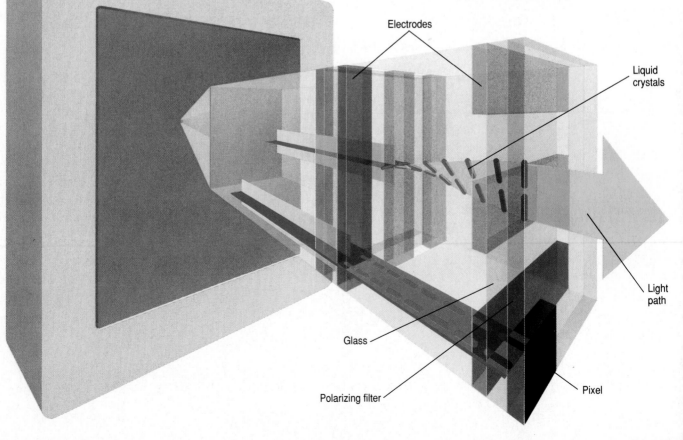

Electrodes

Liquid crystals

Light path

Glass

Pixel

Polarizing filter

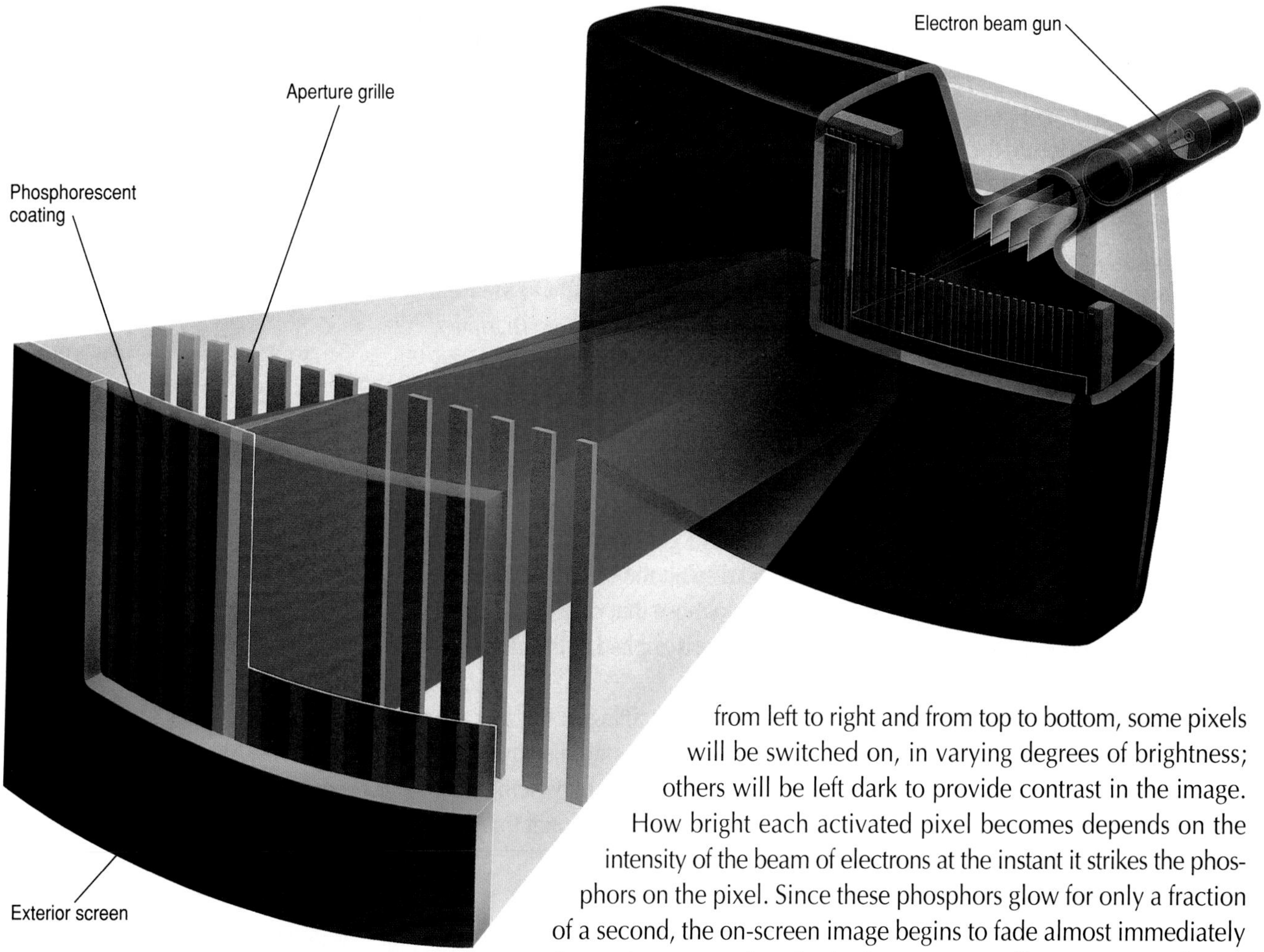

Electron beam gun

Aperture grille

Phosphorescent
coating

Exterior screen

CATHODE RAY TUBE

The CRT shown here is a single-gun three-beam color display system. The gun fires a stream of electrons toward the phosphorescent material on the inside of the screen.

from left to right and from top to bottom, some pixels will be switched on, in varying degrees of brightness; others will be left dark to provide contrast in the image. How bright each activated pixel becomes depends on the intensity of the beam of electrons at the instant it strikes the phosphors on the pixel. Since these phosphors glow for only a fraction of a second, the on-screen image begins to fade almost immediately and must be constantly refreshed—most typically 60 times each second—by a new burst of electrons.

A color CRT works in much the same way as its black-and-white counterpart. Most color CRTs have three electron guns, although single-gun color monitors are also quite common. In either case, the guns generate three electron beams, one to excite each of three colors—red, green or blue—in phosphorescent cells on the pixels covering the back of the screen. A perforated shadow mask or aperture grille behind the screen allows each beam to strike only the corresponding colored phosphors. Depending on the strength of the beam, the phosphors will glow in varying intensities of red, green or blue, producing a full-color image on the screen. The three colors used may not seem impressive, but mixing them together like paints on a palette can produce as many as 16 million hues.

The technology for the slender screens commonly found on portable and laptop computers is no less impressive. These machines need screens that take up far less space than a CRT. With a thickness of three inches or less, their monitors have no bulky glass tubes, no electron guns and no electromagnetic yokes. Instead, the screens have pixels that either darken or lighten in response to electrical signals generated by the display controller. A grid of electrodes defines the location of every pixel; each can be activated by sending an electrical charge to its row and column coordinates.

speed and high resolution of ink-jet printers makes them especially well suited to producing color graphics. Using a print head with four ink nozzles, the printers draw their ink from separate reservoirs containing cyan, magenta, yellow and black inks—from which they can produce a virtually infinite range of hues.

Even greater resolution—and greater speed—can be achieved by a laser printer that generates an entire page at once. A laser beam draws the image of the page onto photosensitive material, and the image is then transferred onto paper. The invention of laser printing, coupled with the advent of high-definition monitors, paved the way for the development of desktop publishing and has also helped to propel computer graphics into realms that go far beyond simple pie charts and bar graphs.

FRACTAL DIMENSIONS

Thanks to computer graphics, scientists can conjure up a world warmed by greenhouse gases. Architects can design and construct their buildings without ever breaking ground. Surgeons can examine diseased tissue before laying a glove on a patient. Molecular biologists can render the invisible visible, unraveling the double-helix structure of DNA, for example, or uncovering the secrets of such distant phenomena as cosmic jets. The computer's graphics skills are also being employed in more down-to-earth ways in computer-aided design and computer-aided manufacturing, transforming mere drawing-boards into high-tech workstations.

Yet no matter what form they take, or how magical they appear, computer graphics are entirely mathematical, the result of thousands of individual equations that turn the binary language of the computer into shapes, colors, reflections and shadows. Early attempts at computer graphics were relatively crude, but advances in the field have been astonishing. Simple two- and three-dimensional images call for relatively unsophisticated equations, but a branch of mathematics called fractal geometry, established by the French mathematician Benoît Mandelbrot in 1975, employs more complex calculations, and produces far more refined images. A fractal is a visual representation of a mathematical equation designed to break down and quantify irregular geometrical shapes, both natural and man-made. Frac-

THE GRAPHICS THRESHOLD

Computer-generated graphics are having an impact in the arts as well as the sciences. The small illustration is a fractal image made with an IBM 3090-600E supercomputer at the Cornell National Supercomputer Facility. The image at right, Forest Devil's Moon Night, *was created in 1989 by sculptor Kenneth Snelson using a powerful workstation and a three-dimensional animation software package similar to those used in scientific imaging and for many TV animated computer images.*

tal geometry can be used to represent such naturally occurring irregular shapes as curving lines and wrinkled surfaces, clouds and snowflakes, mountain ranges and branching trees. Used as a building block of computer graphics, fractals give the computer the ability to depict the natural world with convincing realism, creating complex large-scale shapes made up of identical or similar shapes on a small scale, repeated many times over.

AN ORCHESTRA IN A BOX

Breaking a larger whole into its component parts is also at the root of computer music and sound synthesis. The earliest synthesizers rocked out of the laboratory and into the recording studio in the 1960s. These were analog devices that worked by feeding electrical current through a series of oscillators, filters and amplifiers. The result, still in the form of electrical signals, could then be channeled to a loudspeaker, which translated the electrical signals it received into the pressure waves that the human ear perceives as sound.

But first-generation synthesizers, like early computers, could only be reprogrammed by being completely rewired. Changing the sound output meant physically changing the settings of the synthesizer's myriad dials and switches, a process that could take hours of dial-tweaking and switch-throwing to produce just a few seconds of synthesized sound.

That sort of tedium became obsolete in the early 1980s when the analog synthesizer was replaced by a digital version. Not only can a digital synthesizer store hundreds of programmed sounds, any one of which can be retrieved at the touch of a button, but it can also record, store and replay as music virtually any known sound—whether the crack of shattering glass, the lilt of a human voice or the strains of a Stradivarius. The sound can even be transposed and replayed in a different key at the press of a button. The source of the machine's versatility is that it understands music not as modified electrical current, but as strings of binary ones and zeros—the universal language of the computer.

Despite the common language, merging the sound-generating abilities of the synthesizer with the sound-processing skills of the computer was not as simple as it might have seemed. The two kinds of machines lacked a suitable connection, or interface. Without such a device, there was no way to transmit digitized musical notes from a particular electronic instrument to the computer, or vice versa. Moreover, the lack of a uniform timing standard meant that an electronic instrument built by one manufacturer could not be synchronized with any instrument made by another manufacturer.

All that changed in 1983 when the major manufacturers of keyboard synthesizers agreed on a common specification for data transmission and exchange. That specification, called the Musical Instrument Digital Interface, or MIDI, allowed a computer equipped with the hardware to act as a kind of switchboard linking all kinds of digital electronic instruments—including keyboards, drum machines and guitar synthesizers.

MIDI also dictated how that data would be structured. According to the rules governing the system, every message consists of three bytes. The first byte alerts the receiving instrument that a note must be turned on or off. Next come two data bytes, one to tell the instrument exactly which note to turn on or off, and the other to indicate how the specified note should be played, whether loudly or softly, sustained or staccato.

A single piece of music, depending on its length, might be made up of hundreds or thousands of MIDI messages. Bytes travel serially, or one at a time, and since MIDI standards set the normal transmission rate at 31,259 bits per second, approximately 3,900 bytes can zip through a MIDI music system every second—a speed that is adequate for most applications. Four different modes further coordinate the flow of electronic traffic over MIDI's 16 available channels, allowing a master keyboard to cue individual electronic instruments, telling them exactly which notes to play and when to play them.

MIDI's role as maestro in an electronic orchestra is further enhanced by dedicated software that can turn an ordinary personal computer—usually connected to a specialized keyboard—into the digital equivalent of a multitrack tape deck of the kind used in professional recording studios. With such specialized software, a musician can use a computer's internal and storage memory units to record digitized music. Separate tracks can then be laid down as needed, turning a lone musician into a veritable one-man band. The same software will allow the musician to go back and correct any mistakes or to transpose entire passages of music at a keystroke and print out the written score.

The home studio shown below can produce the same music and sound effects as a professional 24-track recording studio. The computer acts as the main sequencer for the system, which includes MIDI hardware, three sound generators, a mixing board and a reel-to-reel tape recorder.

MIDI Magic

The days when a rock group walked onstage and simply played its greatest hits are long gone. Concert fans have come to expect the level of sophistication in live performances that they hear on tapes and compact disks. With the help of computers, onstage musicians now can produce shows—from one-person acoustic performances to massive rock and roll extravaganzas—that sound almost as good as their studio efforts.

Just as it transformed studio recording technology, Musical Instrument Digital Interface, or MIDI, has fundamentally changed live performances. A lone performer, using only a guitar or keyboard, can control other instruments and create a variety of sounds. A MIDI interpreter acts as middleman. When the performer hits certain triggers, perhaps specific notes or keyboard positions, other auxiliary keyboards are activated. Complex networks connecting many instruments can be established to create multilayered music. Background vocals, instrumentals and sound effects can kick in at exactly the right moment. Everything is synchronized and cued through MIDI; even visual effects can be added to the system.

When a band tours, it performs in many venues, each with unique acoustics that alter sound in different ways. But amplifiers can be electronically preprogrammed to compensate for conditions in locales that are less than ideal—stadiums, hockey rinks or old halls. The characteristics of the sound are tailored precisely for optimum clarity and level. Onstage monitoring systems are programmed and cued for specific performers and songs. If a singer lacks vocal power, for example, the amplification system can compensate. Vocal range and power are electronically restored by the time the sound reaches the audience.

Ironically, so many studio techniques are now used in concert that musicians and sound technicians often go to great lengths to make the performances sound less precise and more "live." Even spontaneity, it seems, must be carefully planned.

By relying on advanced electronic recording techniques, the four-member rock group Pink Floyd, *pictured in performance above, can create a multilayered wall of sound. In concert they are able to reproduce their unique recorded sound by using additional performers and an elaborate computerized sound setup.*

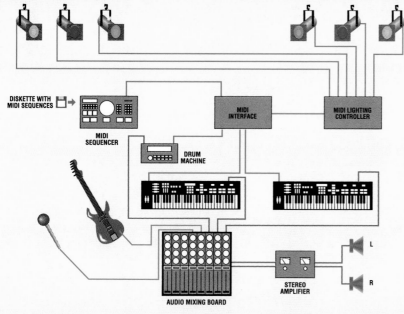

DISKETTE WITH
MIDI SEQUENCES

MIDI
SEQUENCER

DRUM
MACHINE

MIDI
INTERFACE

MIDI LIGHTING
CONTROLLER

AUDIO MIXING BOARD

STEREO
AMPLIFIER

L

R

WIRED FOR SOUND

This simplified schematic shows a very basic MIDI-computer system that could be used in a concert. A preprogrammed sequencer, drum machine, two synthesizers and special effects lighting are all linked directly and coordinated through a MIDI interface device. The microphone and guitar are connected to the audio mixing board, which is controlled by a technician.

An FBI artist uses photographs of family members to age an image of a missing child. While the image-processing software makes this work possible, the skills and experience of the human operator are central to the procedure.

On the opposite page, the photograph at near right is of Christopher, age five. The image at far right shows how he may look at age eight, based on known child growth patterns and photographs of other members of his family.

Mature Considerations

In a hypothetical but true-to-life scenario, a five-year-old child called Christopher has disappeared in an apparent kidnapping. Three years later, the child is still missing. Local police and the FBI circulate regular nationwide bulletins with his description, along with a number to call if he is spotted. And although no known photograph has been taken of him in the three years since his abduction, the bulletins also include an updated picture of Christopher—an image that is possible thanks to a computer program that helps FBI artists accurately predict how a person will look as he grows older.

Since a child's face changes more quickly than an adult's, even a short lapse of time may render existing photographs out-of-date. But a well-established knowledge of human growth patterns and certain other important clues allow a trained computer artist to predict, with a high degree of accuracy, what any five-year-old would look like long after he disappeared, even reaching forward into his adolescent and adult years.

In this example, to help create the face of Christopher as he might appear at the age of eight, the FBI would work with photographs of his parents at the same age, as well as pictures of the child and his siblings. In such cases, a computer artist studies all photos and then interviews the parents to select which of the images most resemble their child. The best photos of Christopher and his most similar looking relative—in this case his mother, Jean, at age eight—would be scanned into the computer. The program establishes a grid for each image and the two are overlaid and lined up at the pupils. Then, some of Christopher's features would be replaced by his mother's older ones.

Normally, the lower half of a child's face grows more quickly than the upper; in this case the artist chose to use Jean's stronger chin as a model. At the same time Christopher's distinctive eyes were aged without reference to his mother's. The program then stretches the image to simulate the changes in facial and skull structure that normally occur as a child grows. The computer artist may also use electronic tools to add shadows and select updated hairstyles and clothing. What evolves as the final image of an eight-year-old Christopher is actually a skillful composite of real features from Jean, statistical knowledge about how children's faces age and artistic interpretation.

FBI computer artists say their program is much faster—and 10 times more accurate—than previous manual methods. However, no such system can automatically age a missing person's face without error; nor do updated photographs guarantee that a child will be located.

MAKING CONNECTIONS

By linking computers together, over long distances or short, users create networks that allow them to pool their own talents and the resources of their computers. To link computers by means of a telephone line, a device known as a modem is the indispensable connection. Shorthand for modulator-demodulator, a modem modulates, or changes, a computer's binary output into the analog signals the telephone system transmits. On the receiving end, the device demodulates the analog signals, converting them back into a digital form intelligible to the receiving computer. The modem hardware unit can either be built into the computer or added on later by means of a plug-in circuit board. Alternatively, a modem can take the form of a separate, external device that plugs into the computer and into nearby telephone and electrical outlets. Manufacturers are including built-in modems as standard equipment in increasing numbers of home computers.

Modems are classified by speed—the fastest rate at which a given machine can transmit or receive data, measured in bits per second, or bps. Low-speed modems, which use a slow but reliable technique called frequency-shift keying, transmit or receive data at speeds of up to 600 bps. Most of today's modems operate at medium speeds—from 1,200 to 2,400 bps—using a faster technique called phase-key shifting. High-speed modems relying on even more sophisticated modulation techniques can transmit anywhere from 4,800 to 9,600 bps.

NETWORKING

The four computers linked by the red lines are part of a local area network, or LAN. The LAN computers need no special interface to exchange information. Each LAN computer may be connected to distant computers over telephone lines in a wide area network, or WAN. The standalone modem device acts as a digital-to-analog interface between the LAN computers and the distant computer on the blue line.

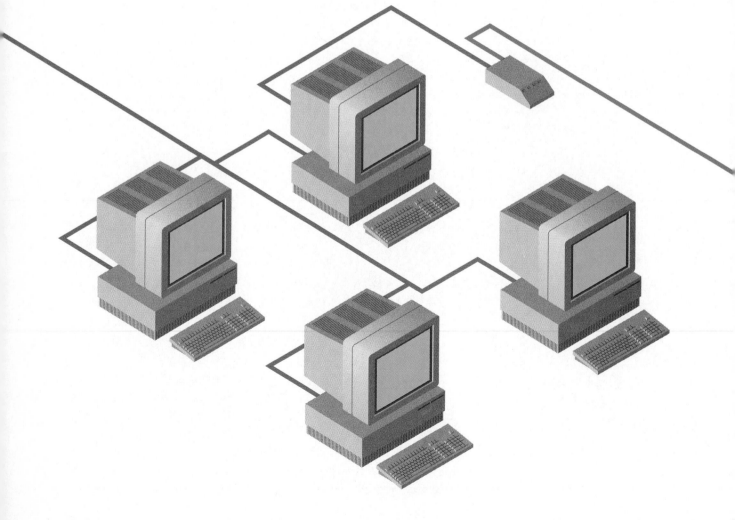

To link computers in far-flung corners of the globe—forming a wide-area network, or WAN—integration of satellites and cables designed to handle data is necessary. Computers within a smaller area—a single building, for instance, or a single office site—can be linked physically, via fiber-optic cable (which carries information in the form of light) or by copper wire, coaxial cables or telephone lines to create a local area network, or LAN. It is even possible to join a combination of LANs and WANs to form a single network. The most extensive is Internet, a sprawling mega-network whose tentacles stretch to 35 countries, encompassing 936 separate networks and some 175,000 computers.

Networks enable their users to exchange information and give them access to the resources and services of remote databases and electronic bulletin boards. However, different computers often have incompatible hardware designs or processing techniques, a fact of electronic life that dictates the need for special communications software to permit dialogue between computers.

Some network cables use the broadband method of transmission, which allows the simultaneous transmission of multiple signals by subdividing the cable into multiple channels and using a technique called multiplexing. Most cables, however, use the baseband method, in which all signals travel one at a time over a single channel. To keep data packets from two computers from colliding with one another on the same cable, the communications program relies on one of two access methods. In the first, called carrier sensing, a transmitting node checks the cable before commandeering it for its own use. If it senses a carrier, or signal, on the line—in effect, getting a busy signal—the node must wait until the cable clears. The second access method, token passing, uses a binary token as a kind of electronic admission ticket. The token is passed from node to node for a specified length of time, during which only the node holding the token is allowed access to the cable and can transmit data.

ONE WAY TO THE GLOBAL VILLAGE

Computers are fast fulfilling media guru Marshall McLuhan's quarter-century-old prophecy that the world would one day evolve into a single global village. Some degree of cultural globalization is already under way, with microwave links for telephone connections and live television news coverage of revolutions, wars, sporting events and concerts brought into a billion homes at once. As all categories of information are digitized and sent around the planet at the speed of light, the financial, social and geopolitical implications can only be guessed at. With an eye toward this globalization of information, telephone companies have been developing a worldwide communications system called the Integrated Services Digital Network, designed to replace the present-day analog telephone system. The goal of ISDN is to produce a single world standard for transmitting and receiving digitized information, from telephone calls to financial transactions and television broadcasts. Such a network would employ fiber-optic cables on the ground and communications satellites parked in geo-stationary orbit 22,000 miles above the Equator. Eventually this could link every business and household computer in the world into a single system.

Already on-line in Britain, France, Japan and parts of the United States, ISDN functions like a telecommunications superhighway, speeding the simultaneous transmission of voice, data and images over multiple channels. The core—literally—of the operation is a fiber-optic cable. This hair-thin strand of glass carries information that has been converted into pulses of light. The pulses, each corresponding to a bit of information, are generated by light-emitting diodes (LEDs) or by small lasers, which follow instructions from a computer. Transmission rates have doubled annually in recent years. LEDs emit pulses—or bits per second—in the millions, while lasers can generate billions of bits per second.

Telephone systems currently consist of land lines (using a mixture of fiber-optics and copper wire), microwave links and satellite communications. The full potential of ISDN will only be realized when the systems use fiber-optics along the entirety of their networks. Two 64,000-bps voice channels and one 16,000-bps data channel are currently used to form the backbone of a basic ISDN system. A 100 per cent fiber-optic ISDN could substantially increase those speeds to perhaps as much as one trillion bits per second.

Even without ISDN the world is already intricately connected electronically through facsimile machines, cellular telephones, automatic bank teller machines, electronic mail and computer networks. It has become commonplace for travelers to access their bank accounts from the other side of the globe. Every day thousands of telephone calls are routinely placed from aircraft 35,000 feet high, cruising at 600 miles per hour, with the cost automatically charged to a credit card account on the ground. An airline passenger can send a fax to a moving car without giving it a second thought, or even call home to a "smart" VCR, instructing it to record a broadcast six months in the future.

ISDN systems and their successors are expected to further speed the development of increasingly sophisticated electronic hardware. Consumer products will include units that combine high definition television and computer technology in a hybrid called a smart TV. Such a device could act as an electronic sentinel, scanning the digital airwaves and automatically recording any programs of interest to its owner, basing its decisions upon established viewing patterns. Supported by the right software, a smart TV might also function as an "agent," a software secretary that acts on its owner's behalf to track down desired information, to weed out unwanted intrusions, and even to prioritize incoming electronic mail.

LONG-DISTANCE DIAGNOSIS

ISDN is also expected to foster the development of telemedicine. This new approach to the art of healing combines the benefits of computer graphics and networking with the practice of medical diagnosis. In doing so, it promises to give even the remotest rural hospitals instant access to the resources of the world's finest metropolitan medical centers.

Telemedicine's potential was dramatically demonstrated in early 1989 in the wake of a devastating earthquake in Soviet Armenia. In an effort to cope with the medical aftershocks of the quake, four American medical institutions were linked

THE GLOBAL VILLAGE
Information is transmitted around the world using a variety of techniques. A digital message may be converted to analog and sent through regular telephone lines (blue) or it may be sent in digital form via fiber-optic cables (red). Digital microwave and satellite links (yellow) are used for data, voice and image transmission, with satellite uplinks typically used to transmit television images.

by NASA satellite to Armenian hospitals and rehabilitation centers. This computer network, called Telemedicine Spacebridge, allowed doctors in Armenia to beam X-rays, diagnostic scans and other data to U.S. doctors, who reviewed each case and recommended appropriate treatments and long-term therapies. A few months later, in June 1989, the system was put to the test again after a massive explosion in Siberia destroyed two trains, injuring or killing more than a thousand passengers. In both instances, Telemedicine Spacebridge performed so effectively that NASA officials subsequently earmarked the system as a prototype for a network that might one day be put into action to cope with medical emergencies aboard a planned U.S. space station.

In the meantime, back on Earth, graphics networks called Pictorial Archiving and Communications Systems are further streamlining the practice of medicine by computerizing the central files of radiology departments. With PACS, images can be stored indefinitely, retrieved as needed from any computer in the network, and even reformatted to create three-dimensional views that can be rotated to give a physician a clearer perspective of a particular pathology.

Similar systems are integrating the output of a battery of medical imaging systems with patient information records to create a comprehensive diagnostic database. These ID/PACS, for Integrated Diagnostics/PACS, give physicians access to an electronic medical file, including the results of diagnostic information generated by computer and X-ray scanning of the patient. If need be, such a file can

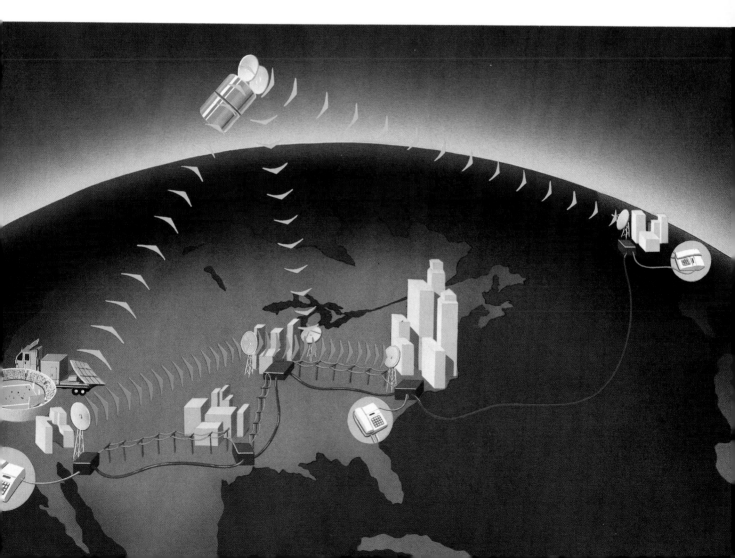

be transmitted via satellite—at a speed of up to one million bits per second—to another hospital for review by other specialists. Alternatively, using a new device, X-rays can be laser-scanned and transmitted from doctor to doctor over ordinary telephone lines. At the receiving end, the digitized X-ray can be printed on X-ray film or called up and displayed on a monitor.

One drawback of such systems, however, is the problem of storing the hundreds of millions of data bytes generated daily by a single major hospital. The solution may take the form of an optical disk "jukebox" containing 100 or so erasable optical disks, each of which can hold several billion bytes, or gigabytes, of data. Linking several of these jukeboxes together would result in a massive storage memory that could handle the output of the world's largest hospitals.

Telemedicine is only one example of the impact computers are having on the medical profession. Indeed expert systems, which mimic the reasoning power of a physician, have become a mainstay in other hospital departments, turning the computer into an electronic specialist that is always on call, always ready to nudge its human counterpart toward a correct diagnosis or to suggest a course of treatment. In some instances, most notably in calculating drug dosages, the electronic specialist is more accurate than its human colleagues. Some "narrow-margin" medications, for example, are effective only within a very limited spectrum. At dosage levels even slightly below the spectrum, some drugs may not work at all. At levels slightly above, the drug might be so toxic that it threatens the patient's life. Given that risk, drug-dosage software has the potential to be a lifesaver and is, in fact, already revolutionizing patient care.

THE IMPETUS OF THE SPACE PROGRAM

When the history of the computer age is written, both the military and the space program will be seen as key players. Wartime computers were put to work on code-breaking and weapons design; ENIAC was a response to the U.S. Army's need for more accurate artillery firing tables during World War II. And although the war was over before ENIAC was completed, the machine subsequently earned its stripes as part of the team that built the first hydrogen bomb. Just as there would have been no exploration of space without computers, it is unlikely that computers would have come as far as they have without the peacetime boost of the space program. The computers that guided early piloted flights into orbit were ground-based, and it was not until the first Gemini mission in 1965 that a digital computer went along for the ride as onboard navigator and guidance-control officer.

Since the 1969 moon landing, spacecraft have mapped Venus and probed Mars, skirted the rings of Saturn and headed beyond the bounds of the Solar System. In the process they have beamed back volumes of data and shed new light on the mysteries of the universe. Indeed, by 1983, the Infrared Astronomy Satellite had surveyed the entire sky at infrared wavelengths and detected at least 10,000 galaxies not previously seen from Earth. Most exciting of all, perhaps, were the planetary pilgrimages of the twin Voyager probes, which were launched separately in 1977 and completed their scheduled flybys of Jupiter and Saturn between 1979 and 1981. Its mission accomplished, Voyager 1 then hurtled at speeds up to 65,000 miles per hour toward a rendezvous, a half million years from now, with the Constellation Ophiuchus.

The Magnetic Resonance Imaging system scans a patient in "slices." By stacking the slices, three-dimensional images are built up, allowing doctors to make diagnoses without intrusive techniques.

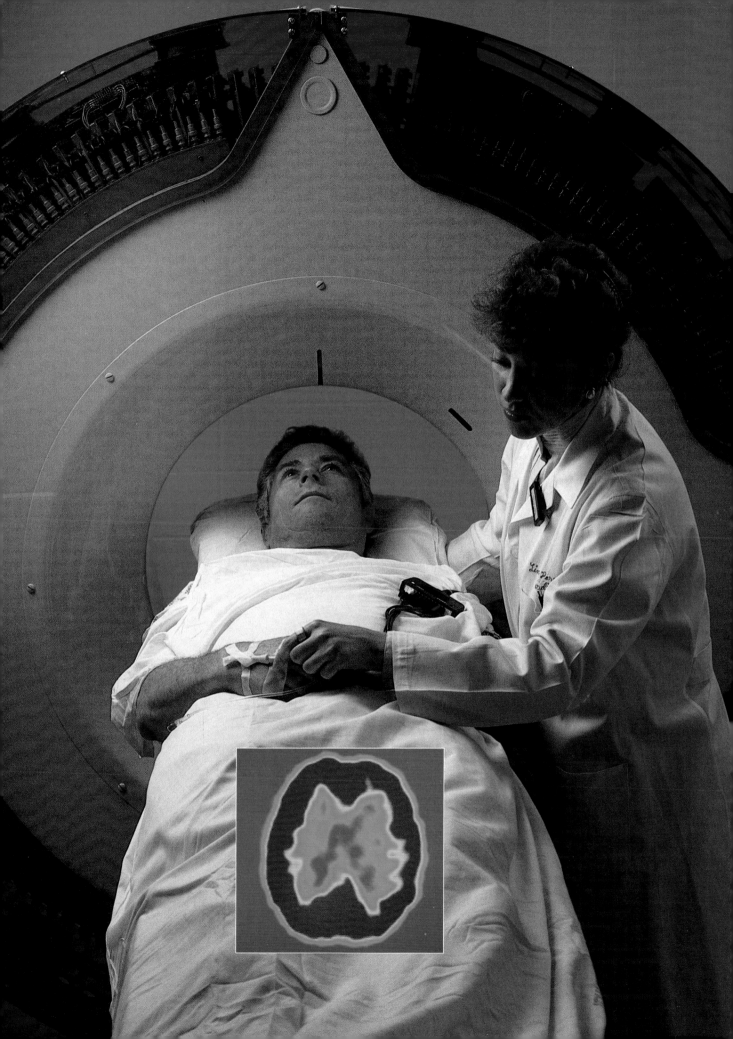

For Voyager 2, however, Jupiter and Saturn were just whistle-stops on a grand tour of the outer planets. NASA engineers, eager to take advantage of an alignment of Jupiter, Saturn, Uranus and Neptune that occurs only once every 176 years, revised the probe's itinerary. By using one planet's gravity as a kind of slingshot, engineers could propel Voyager 2 outward without spending too much precious fuel. Throughout its journey, the probe looked for guidance to a command-control computer that by today's standards would be regarded as primitive.

PHOTOGRAPHING COAL BY STARLIGHT

Of all the information gathered by Voyager 2, it was the photographs that most captured the public's imagination. Obtaining pictures of the methane-blackened moons of Uranus, and of Neptune, which receives just 1/1,000 of the sunlight that falls on Earth, was a feat one scientist likened to "photographing coal by starlight." An onboard computer divided each image taken by Voyager's two cameras into 640,000 pixels and then measured the brightness of each one, translating the data into ones and zeros.

A microwave transmitter sent this stream of bits at the speed of light—in a journey lasting hours—to one of the three huge dish antennas on Earth that constitute the Deep Space Network. Once received, the faint signals were boosted and relayed via satellite to the Jet Propulsion Laboratory in Pasadena, California. There, computers converted the bits back to pixels, and the resulting images were com-

Computers on board the space probe Voyager 1 digitized a photograph of the planet Saturn, sending the information back to Earth as a stream of data bits. The image was reconverted (below), *and then computer enhanced* (right) *to show greater detail and resolution.*

bined through red, green and blue filters to create full-color photographs. As Voyager went deeper into space, scientists devised a technique called image-data compression to reduce the number of bits that had to be transmitted to the ground stations. Rather than sending the brightness value for each pixel, the computer forwarded only the difference in brightness levels between adjacent pixels, cutting the number of bits —and the power needed to transmit them—by 75 percent. With Neptune behind it, Voyager 2 is now adrift in space. Sometime around the year 2015, its plutonium generators will at last sputter out, even as the tiny craft nears the heliopause, the edge of the solar system and the beginning of interstellar space.

From there, the ghost ship will sail on into an endless night, its cameras forever darkened, its transmitters stilled. But the probe will carry a message: a copper-plated audiovisual disk designed to survive undamaged for a billion years. Recorded on this electronic testament from Earth are greetings in 60 different languages as well as such disparate sounds as the chirp of a cricket, a sample of 20th Century rock 'n' roll, the song of a humpback whale and a Bach concerto. Also encoded on the disk are the image of a snowflake and the vision of a human infant nursing at its mother's breast.

Aboard, too, for any who might encounter the craft and wish to plumb its secrets, are the electronic marvels that made it possible for the probe to be such a splendid proxy for human explorers. Some future extraterrestrial archaeologist may spend a lifetime of rewarding study with Voyager's computers.

Future Considerations

When IBM entered the burgeoning personal computer market in 1981—late to join the fray—its presence gave the field a new level of credibility. By 1990, the corporate giant had sold off its famed typewriter division, once the symbol of IBM worldwide. There could have been no more telling sign that the computer age had fully and irrevocably arrived.

The pace of change since the first functioning computers were designed during the years of World War II has been astonishing. In 1950 there were under 100 computers in existence; by 1970 they numbered 50,000. Now 50,000 are manufactured in a day. And as computers become smaller, cheaper and more powerful, their number will increase dramatically. Chip manufacturers consistently outstrip what were once considered optimistic predictions as to how many switches can be crammed into an integrated circuit. As a result, the processing power of a million-dollar mainframe of 20 years ago can now be purchased in a laptop package for less than $5,000.

It is tempting to think that this pace cannot be maintained, that the innovation must soon abate. Yet there are no such indications. But in which direction dramatic new changes will lead, and from where the innovations will come, is often uncertain. One expert likened the situation to a Greek temple builder's trying to predict the future of civil engineering without a knowledge of concrete, steel or the arch.

Development will continue in some known areas, among them materials, processes and applications. New substances have frequently been billed as the heirs-apparent to silicon, yet none of them have panned out. Now it appears that silicon will continue to play a dominant role in most standard computers—it still represents the ideal for mass chipmaking. But experts believe that new materials will be used—in some cases in conjunction with silicon, in others by blazing new trails. Superconductors, which received so much publicity during the 1980s, will not be found in computers for many years. Still, they hold great promise and remain the focus of research.

There is one absolute limit to how fast binary information can be processed: the speed of light. The only way to reach it is by replacing electrons, the basic units of electricity, with photons, the building blocks of light. At least one functioning prototype for optical computers already exists; commercial versions may be on the distant horizon by the turn of the century.

Few disciplines remain untouched by computers. Even art and music have been changed fundamentally by digital technology. Of the infinite applications conceived for computers, however, perhaps the most intriguing and controversial is artificial intelligence. Even now, there are dedicated computers—essentially electronic savants—making decisions on specific subjects. But a machine that makes a series of logical choices through an unhindered process of reasoning remains the ultimate goal.

According to a recent survey of dozens of the world's most renowned computer experts, the future of computing will be one of innovation and breakthroughs. In 1989, no less an authority than programming pioneer retired Rear Admiral Grace Hopper commented that if computers were airplanes, they would be at the DC-2 stage. "We're only at the beginning. We haven't half got started yet."

WHICH WAY TO THE FUTURE?
The future path of computing may not be a straight one, but it holds much bright promise. New materials, processes and applications will undoubtedly make life easier and more convenient, but will not come effortlessly or cheaply.

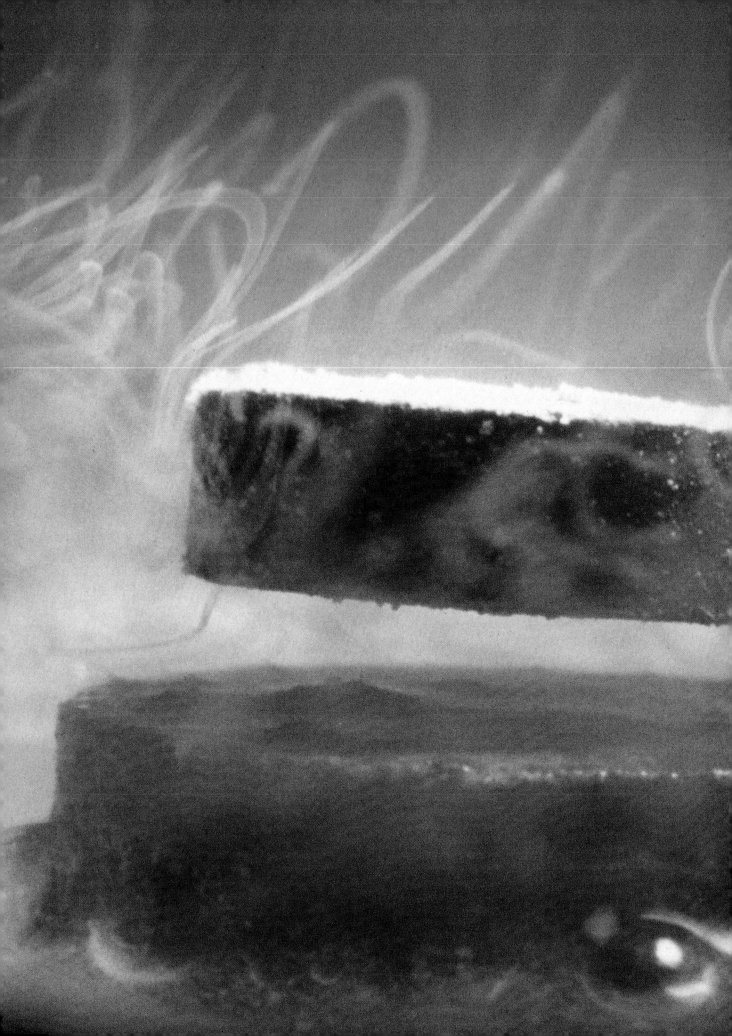

Without silicon, there would have been no revolution in microelectronics. Luckly, the element—the main ingredient in sand—is as abundant in nature as it is suited for shuttling electrons through the pathways of an integrated circuit. Moreover, it is a durable and malleable substance. Wafers of silicon chips stand up well, without buckling, under rigorous mass-production conditions. Yet since the mid-1970s, industry experts have been predicting that silicon's days are numbered, that the material is nearing its useful limits: No more switches can be integrated, no more speed culled, from the already minuscule circuitry. But every year the industry produces faster, more powerful silicon chips and ever-smaller circuitry.

Clearly, silicon will continue to drive computing well into the next century, but other materials are, in fact, gaining fast. In 1990, for example, an experimental microchip that combined silicon and a small amount of the element germanium was unveiled by IBM. The company claimed that, under ideal conditions, its individual transistors could switch 1,000 times faster than other silicon-based chips. Gallium arsenide (GaAs), a compound that has been heralded since the mid-1980s as silicon's successor, also may increase speed. All things being equal—switch speed, for example—electrons move through GaAs six to seven times faster than through silicon, yet require less power to do so. And at high temperatures, GaAs chips, unlike those made from silicon, do not begin to malfunction. But gallium is rare—only 0.01 percent of the Earth's crust—and expensive. It is also fragile; wafers of GaAs chips are less pliable than silicon wafers and fracture more easily.

Despite the disadvantages, GaAs chips will be at the heart of new supercomputers such as the Cray-3, and are already employed by the military. But it will take the development of new mass-manufacturing techniques before GaAs microchips become even half as commonplace as their silicon forerunners.

While GaAs will be used increasingly in computer systems over the next decade, the wait will be longer before another group of highly touted materials—superconductors—achieve widespread application. The phenomena of superconductivity allows electrons to pass through certain substances with virtually no resistance. If applied to microchip circuitry, this property could allow computers to be extremely fast while generating no heat. Until the mid-1980s, such materials were known to work only at extremely low temperatures—typically at minus 418° Fahrenheit. It is prohibitively expensive to cool computer circuitry to that degree. But with the development of "high temperature" superconductors that work at up to minus 292° Fahrenheit, superconducting computers begin to become more feasible.

Superconducting materials are now being used on an experimental basis in spy satellites, but experts do not see a practical application in microchips until well into the next century. Etching circuits into the thin superconducting films without compromising their remarkable conductive powers is one challenge. And cooling mechanisms necessary for such circuitry will continue to be an expensive proposition. In the meantime, researchers continue the search for higher temperature superconductors.

SILICON'S SUCCESSOR?

A magnet levitating above a disk of superconductive material has become a symbol for superconductivity. Because there would be little resistance to electrons in a superconductive circuit, computers may one day contain millions of switches, yet consume no more electricity than a flashlight.

The machine looks nothing like today's elegantly packaged microcomputers. Just under a foot high and two feet square, it is an unwieldy collection of prisms, mirrors, lenses and metal fittings. And its performance is hardly earth-shattering: There is no permanent memory; it is only capable of simple arithmetic; and its 128 switches have a maximum speed of one million operations per second—slower than a personal computer. Crude perhaps, but the world's first digital optical processor may be as much a milestone in computing as was the first primitive integrated circuit.

The idea of computing with light—using photons instead of electrons—has been both hotly pursued and cruelly ridiculed since the late 1950s. When lasers were invented a few years later, a flurry of research was directed toward developing a machine that could activate a computer's on-off switches with beams of light. Then interest waned; light computers seemed to belong in the world of science fiction. By the 1980s, research had intensified again, and in early 1990, Alan Huang, a research scientist with AT&T Bell Laboratories in Short Hills, New Jersey, unveiled a digital processor—not quite a computer—that used beams of light and gallium arsenide switches, called S-Seeds, to process information.

Many experts believe that Huang's machine will intensify the worldwide effort to develop a full-fledged optical computer. In the optical processor, lenses focus and direct lasers toward mirrors that become either reflective or opaque, thus redirecting or absorbing the light to create the ones and zeros of digital computing. With this technology, a more advanced optical computer could be 1,000 times faster than today's electronic computers.

Such speed and power is possible because of the unique properties of light. Photons travel about 10 times faster than electrons. But more important, they do not need to move along wires and can intersect without interference. Thus a massive and complex interconnectivity between switches can be established, making possible enormous neural networks that mimic the brain.

It is unlikely that a functioning optical computer will be available commercially by the turn of the century, but widespread applications are already envisaged. One short-term possibility will see light-based computers connect directly into fiber-optic telephone lines, eliminating the need to switch from electronic to optical signals. In the long term, optical computers will lead to artificially intelligent machines and robots that will recognize and process images and sounds.

SEEING THE LIGHT

Photons eventually may replace electrons as the computer's most basic units. Opinion is divided as to the potential of optical computers, but serious research in the field is under way at AT&T's Bell Labs.

The sound is at first entirely inhuman: high-pitched, monotonous and unmarked by pauses. Then, slowly, the tone assumes variety, and natural hesitations begin to separate indecipherable, yet distinct, words. Eventually, the gibberish becomes language—electronic-sounding, to be sure—but unmistakably English and grammatically correct as well.

Learning is clearly in progress here, and the student is a computer. But no one is feeding this machine a program of rigid commands. Instead, it has learned to speak aloud by studying a short English-language transcript and practicing for hours until it produces human-like speech.

This feat of electronic cognitive learning may be a harbinger of things to come in the field of artificial intelligence—the four-decade-long quest to design thinking machines. Using specialized software, the experimental computer processes information through a complex neural network based on the architecture of the human brain. Of course, the brain has billions of neurons joined by trillions of interconnections, and neural network machines comprise merely hundreds of thousands of nodes and millions of interconnections. Still, experimental computers have exhibited a brain-like ability to process analog information, recognize voices and images, and even to speak—unlike their serial processing counterparts. Serial processors take on incredibly complex problems such as playing international-level chess, trading on the stock market and solving differential equations, but they are incapable of performing simple tasks that wouldn't faze a child. Trying to recognize faces, signatures or the difference between spoken words such as "ball" and "bawl" paralyze a serial computer. Neural networks may change that.

The experimental machines of today, although only one four-millionth as powerful as the brain, have proved themselves capable of human-like learning and decision making. In the short term, neural net computers will become more adept at speech and image recognition. In the long term, smart robots will know how to recognize unexpected situations and adjust accordingly.

Certainly, standard computers will always be used to solve mathematically based problems. Ultimately, though, neural network computers may make their biggest contribution by helping to unlock secrets about how the human brain itself works.

NETWORKING

A neuron fires deep within the cerebral cortex in this photograph of a man-made model of the human brain. Neural nets may point the way to a form of artificial intelligence in which computers begin to learn to reason for themselves.

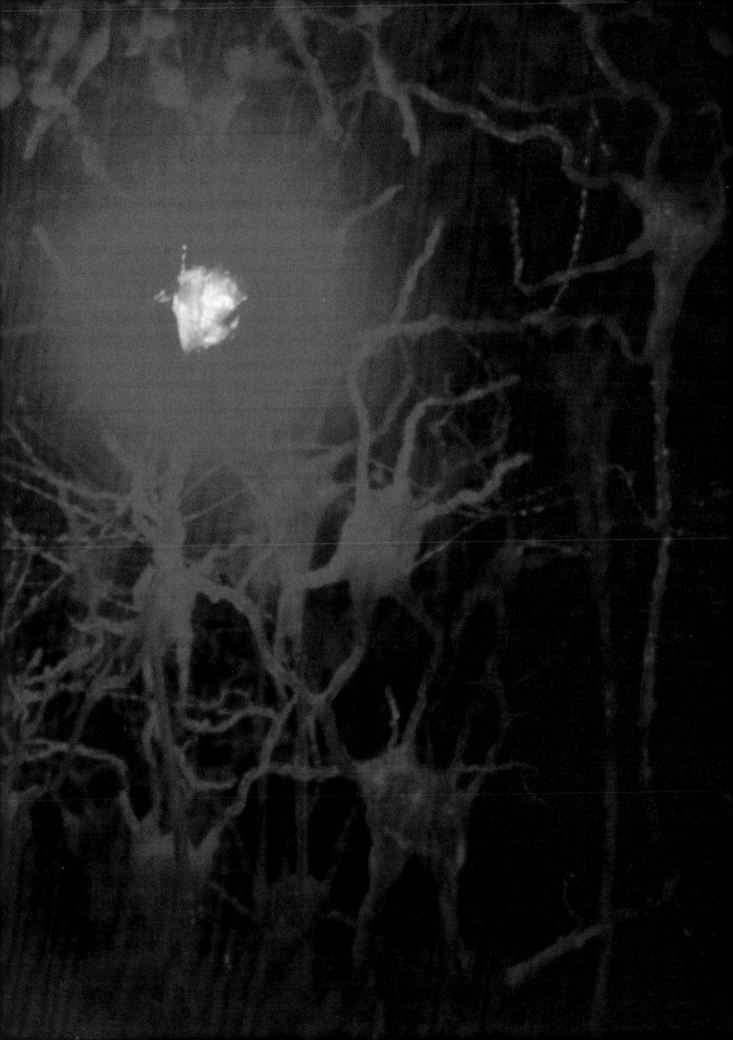

Index

Numerals in *italics* indicate an illustration of the subject mentioned.

PICTURE CREDITS

Multiple credits on a page are read left to right, top to bottom, divided by semicolons.

Cover: Photo illustration by the computer art staff of St. Remy Press.

6 Lawrence Manning/West Light; Courtesy AutoDesk Inc. 7 Cornell National Supercomputer Facility. 8,9 Hans Blohm/Masterfile; Robert Chartier (2); Science Museum Library. 10,11 Science Museum Library (2); Hans Blohm/Masterfile. 12,13 The Computer Museum; Ken Cooper/The Image Bank; Robert Chartier. 14,15 Imtek-Blohm/Masterfile. 16,17 Robert Chartier. 20,21 Robert Chartier. 22,23 Thomas A. Way, courtesy IBM Corporation (4). 25 Thomas A. Way, courtesy IBM Corporation (2). 26,27 Thomas A. Way, courtesy IBM Corporation. 28,29 Thomas A. Way, courtesy IBM Corporation (2). 30,31 Chuck O'Rear/West Light; Steve Dunwell/The Image Bank; Manfred Kage/Peter Arnold Inc. 32,33 Peter Hutchings. 40 Robert Chartier (2). 41 Fred Ward/Black Star (2); Courtesy IBM Corporation. 42,43 Courtesy Delco Electronics (2). 46,47 Les Paparazzi with the kind permission of Danny Green; Robert Chartier; Les Paparazzi with the kind permission of Dawna Golden. 48,49 Mike Dobel/Masterfile. 53 Courtesy Intel Corporation. 56 The Computer Museum; Courtesy Texas Instruments Inc.; Courtesy AT&T Bell Laboratories; Courtesy National Semiconductor. 64,65 Louie Psihoyos/Matrix International. 68,69 Paul Shabroom, courtesy Cray Research Inc.; Courtesy NASA/Ames Research (3). 72,73 Constantine Manos/Magnum Photos. 88 Courtesy AutoDesk Inc. (3). 89 Courtesy DTM Corporation (2). 90,91 Robert Chartier. 94,95 John Paul Endress. 108,109 Dominique Sarraute/The Image Bank. 110,111 Lewis Portnoy/The Stock Market. 116,117 Cornell National Supercomputer Facility; Kenneth Snelson. 119 Courtesy Korg USA. 120,121 Dimo Safari. 122,123 Tom Wolff; Courtesy Carolyn Jackson; Gene O'Donnell, courtesy Federal Bureau of Investigation. 129 Steve Chenn/First Light; Dan McCoy/Rainbow. 130,131 Courtesy United States Geological Survey, Flagstaff, AZ (2). 132,133 Jean-Francois Podeuin/The Image Bank. 134,135 Gabe Palmer/Masterfile. 136,137 Ron Watts/First Light. 138,139 John Allison/Peter Arnold Inc.

ILLUSTRATION CREDITS

18 Claude Lafrance. 28-29 Josée Morin. 38-39 Guy Charette. 66-67 Josée Morin. 74-75 Gilles Beauchemin. 102 Christiane Litalien. 104-105 Guy Charette. 106-107 Claude Lafrance. 112-113 Luc Normandin. 114-115 Sam Montesano. 127 Josée Morin.

ACKNOWLEDGMENTS

The editors wish to thank the following:
Bob Donlan, IBM Corporation, Essex Jct., VT; Donna Cunningham, AT&T Bell Laboratories, Short Hills, NJ; Professor Monroe Newborne, McGill University, Montreal, Que.; Dr. Doyle Knight, Rutgers University, New Brunswick, NJ; Francine Callaghan, Betacom Inc., Montreal, Que.; David Andrea, Office for the Study of Automotive Transportation, University of Michigan, Ann Arbor, MI; Gil Porter and Rob Leggett, Delco Electronics Corporation, Kokomo, IN; John McAfee, Computer Virus Industry Association, Santa Clara, CA; David Schwartz, Mix Magazine, Emryville, CA; Albert Leccese, Audio Analysts, Brossard, Que.; Gene O'Donnell, Federal Bureau of Investigation, Washington, DC; Steven Edwards and David Gertler, Seybold Publications, Media, PA; Tammy Becker, US Geological Survey, Flagstaff, AZ; Thomas A. Way and Sandy Smith, IBM Corporation, Essex Jct., VT; Brian Wallace, The Computer Museum, Boston, MA; Andree DeNiverville, The MacKay Centre, Montreal, Que.; Dr. Val Watson, NASA/Ames Research Center, Moffet Field, CA; Tabatha Jo Bonetti, AutoDesk Inc., Sausalito, CA; Nancy Pressel, Intel Corporation, Santa Clara, CA; Jean-Pierre Provencal, Services Techniques Informatiques, Montreal, Que.; Kent Eckberg, Pioneer Communications of America Inc., Upper Saddle River, NJ; Ron Rundall, 3-M Canada Inc., London, Ont.; Michel Labbe, Apple Canada, Montreal, Que.; Gary Romans, Sony Corporation of America, San Diego, CA; David Benman, VPL Research, Redwood, CA; Kenneth Jones, PMI Limited, Scarborough, Ont.; Jacques Labreche, Interleaf Canada Inc., Montreal, Que.; Randy Whitney, Korg USA, Westbury, NY; Bruce Pollack and Joe Gillio, Sharpe Electronics, Mahwah, NJ; Chau Pham, Sicotel, Mississauga, Ont.; Caroline Horsman, Honda F-1 Racing Team, Langley,UK; Robert L. Gleason and Dr. Rose Anne Fedorko, Federal Bureau of Investigation, Alexandria, West VA.

The following persons also assisted in the preparation of this book:
Shirley Grynspan, Stanley D. Harrison, Jenny Meltzer, Shirley Sylvain.

This book was designed on Apple Macintosh® computers, using QuarkXPress® in conjunction with CopyFlow™ and a Linotronic® 300R for page layout and composition; StrataVision 3d®, Adobe Illustrator 88® and Adobe Photoshop® were used as illustration programs.